Three Mountaintops

An Educator's Adventure Through Destiny

Lemmon Stevenson, Sr.

TO

You are to be Bettye highly commended for the professional services given to our young people and may God continue to bless you forever!

Lemmon Stevenson

12/17/97

Duncan & Duncan, Inc., <u>Publishers</u>

Copyright © 1997 by Lemmon Stevenson, Sr.

Duncan & Duncan, Inc., Publishers
2809 Pulaski Highway,
Address Correspondence to: P.O. Box 1137, Edgewood, MD 21040

Library of Congress Catalog Card Information: 97-69495

Stevenson, Lemmon, May 27, 1928—
   Three Mountaintops: An Educator's Adventure Through Destiny
   1. Autobiography, of Afro-Americans 2. Education 3.
   Afro-American 4. Afro-American life 5. Inspiration/
   Motivation 6. Self-Help

ISBN: 1-878647-43-1

**To order this book from Duncan & Duncan, Inc., please call toll
free 1-800-390-8475, Monday - Friday. Credit cards accepted.**

This book is dedicated to the memory of the students, parents, teachers, and citizens of Mitford School, Elizabeth Heights School, Beck School, Jefferson School, Franklin School, and Rupert School.

iv

Acknowledgments

⁀⅂ he people who did the most to help ensure the writing of this book were my brother-in-law, The Reverend Paul Lawrence Ross; my friend and former attorney, Senator John Martin; my dentist, Dr. Christopher Rohrbach; my wife, Cecile Ross Stevenson; my daughter, Ms. Kathleen Loretta Stevenson Bullock; Mrs. Jane Hamilton, Editor and Director of Word Processing, and the legacy of my subconscious mind which said to me, "You can't do that, or at least no one in your family has ever done it. You will fail for sure! You are not a famous politician, and you do not have any clout. You will need an agent and they are extremely expensive and difficult to get when you are a nobody."

Although I am deeply grateful to a countless number of staunch backers and supporters of this project, Reverend Paul Ross of Charlotte, North Carolina, yelled out to me from his deathbed, "Lemmon, you must write that book. I want you to do it soon! I want to read it."

Senator John Martin said to me, pertaining to a property lawsuit, "Lemmon, could you just explain to me your connections and involvement in the 269 acre Fairfield County, South Carolina, property lawsuit?" I submitted my comments in the form of a letter. He said, "This is a good letter."

Senator Martin is, without question, one of the most honorable, respected, and dedicated humanitarian servants in the state of South Carolina or perhaps the nation. My dentist, best friend, and solid supporter, Dr. Christopher Rohrbach of Pottstown, Pennsylvania, who after reading two-thirds of the book said, "Please hurry up and finish this book. I will buy the first copy published."

Cecile, my wife and childhood sweetheart, read the book and made many invaluable suggestions and corrections. Loretta, my beloved baby daughter and mother of two sons, typed the whole book with the exception of the last section. She accomplished all of this in addition to her human resources responsibilities with the PMA Insurance Company located in King of Prussia, Pennsylvania, her children obligations, church obligations, and many others. Without Loretta's dedicated commitment and untiring support, there would be no book. Mrs. Jane Hamilton, Director of the Word Processing Center, in Pottstown, Pennsylvania, critiqued the entire book. She also typed the last section of the book. She is one of the best editors I know. Her services to this book project were invaluable.

I acknowledge and extend sincere thanks to all of those individuals who made it possible for me to serve as a school administrator in the South Carolina and Pottstown, Pennsylvania, school districts. I am indebted to the building secretaries and faculties of Jefferson School, Franklin School, Rupert School, Dr. Ray E. Feick, former Superintendent; his central staff, and my colleagues. I am extremely grateful and profoundly indebted to the school district's word processing center for hundreds and thousands of letters, memos, speeches, projects, evaluation reports, observations, minutes, along with state and national grant proposals. I simply could not think of any obstacles or challenging tasks that would be equal to the superior performance of the word processing staff. The staff was always available, ready, fully prepared, and willing to do whatever was necessary for anyone—including this migrant from South Carolina. Additionally, I received solid and unwavering support from students, parents, and citizens in all district attendance areas.

Preface

This is a book about the life and the successful career of a man who, from birth, overcame serious obstacles of racial prejudice, financial inadequacy, family circumstances, and a scarcity of educational opportunities. The factual story presented here, in his own words and style, attests to his moral character, intelligence, perseverance, and genuine human attitude toward people. Many of these attributes he learned at an early age from his family who taught him to love and respect all people.

With difficulties described in detail, he managed at an early age to get some schooling. This was the beginning of his ferment belief in himself and that a good education could make his life exciting and worthwhile. He spent his years to maturity realizing this goal. Eventually, he became qualified as a professional in education. He worked as a teacher and school administrator for 45 years.

Since his retirement, Mr. Stevenson, like many other citizens, has watched with much concern the reports of violent behavior, illegal drugs, greed, and general lawlessness, especially among children and young people. Accordingly, he is convinced, almost to an obsession, that quality education of all children and youth is the primary answer for saving America in the 21st Century.

In the following pages, Lemmon Stevenson convincingly puts forth his philosophy and his proven methods for accomplishing this goal. As the story unfolds, one can only admire his sincerity and optimism that *life, liberty and the pursuit of happiness* can be attainable for all Americans.

Fred L. Fowler
Greenville, South Carolina Inter-City School Superintendent, (Retired)

Contents

Foreword

R eading the book *Three Mountaintops* is interesting, compelling, and very characteristic of its author. Lemmon Stevenson is fully committed to helping young people succeed academically, and he has served as their role model.

As Superintendent of the Pottstown School District, I recognized the need to enlist the services of personnel with experience in the process of desegregation and the formulation of an educational program to establish a non-graded instructional curriculum for elementary students. Our goals were to develop an educational plan that would revamp our curriculum to improve academic performance of our minority children, and at the same time, promote racial balance in all six elementary attendance areas.

In our efforts to recruit personnel to assist in this mission, I utilized the services of our recruiting team. This team consisted of one board member, two teachers, one administrator, and the Superintendent. We conducted interviews at two universities in South Carolina. One of the candidates was currently serving as a principal in a newly constructed high school. His credentials were very impressive, and we received out-

standing recommendations from colleges and the Superintendent of Schools.

Our entire recruiting team was impressed with Mr.
Stevenson during his interview. We visited his school and later
that day, visited his home and met his family. Mr. Stevenson
accepted our invitation to visit the Pottstown School District in
Pottstown, PA, and consider an administrative position with the
district. After meeting with teachers, administrators, board members, and citizens of the community, he accepted the principalship
of Jefferson School. Two of our local citizens, John Foster, and
Catherine Beasley, were very helpful in providing housing for
the Stevensons, and a very warm welcome to Pottstown.

Lemmon Stevenson was extremely helpful with our desegregation plans and, when we reorganized the attendance areas of
our schools, he accepted the principalship of Rupert Elementary
School. The building was transformed from 100% Caucasian students, to more than 25% minority students.

In spite of the major organizational change, the Rupert
pupils were on par with their academic performance in a very
short time. Lem solicited the assistance of local business people
and the PTA to promote a 25 station computer lab. Lem scheduled every class to be in the computer lab at least once every
week. The services of an aide were secured to assist the teachers and the pupils. If you called the Rupert School and asked
for Mr. Stevenson, the secretary would almost always say, "Mr.
Stevenson is in the computer lab." Lem enjoyed helping the
teachers and pupils become computer literate.

We were very fortunate to have Lemmon Stevenson come
to Pottstown as an educator, and I feel fortunate to have served
on the same administrative team. He accepted the challenge to
come to Pottstown and contribute his expertise and talents to

come to Pottstown and contribute his expertise and talents to accomplish the mission adopted by the Pottstown School District. I asked Lem to assume tasks which included: Director of Title I; travel with recruiting team; offer a non-graded primary educational program; and provide input for new attendance boundaries. Lem accepted his normal responsibilities and the assigned tasks with enthusiasm. He made very productive contributions in the field of education for the Pottstown School District.

I have known Lemmon Stevenson for 25 years, 19 as his Superintendent. He is truly a family man with strong religious convictions. I encouraged his wife, Cecile, to accept employment as a school teacher in the Boyertown School District. Cecile completed 23 years in this district, and she was highly respected by the parents, staff, and administration.

I am extremely happy to have Lem and his family as very dear friends for one quarter of a century.

Dr. Ray E. Feick, Ed.D.
Former Superintendent, Pottstown
School District, Pottstown, PA

Introduction

S etting honorable, humanitarian, and respectable goals and analyzing and fully evaluating the circumstances pertaining to achieving your chosen goals is the focus of this book. Implementing or demonstrating the necessary commitment, courage, and perseverance to ensure goal success are crucial factors that are also highlighted within these pages.

You will learn why the will to survive and succeed by believing in yourself, never giving in, never giving up, and never giving out no matter how difficult the goals become are the only true determinants for one's success in life!

But most of all, the story you are about to read is in essence about promoting pride, love, and respect for self. It is based on the contention that every human being is uniquely important and must learn how to love and respect self before ever being able to love and respect others. It has been written that we should love our neighbors as ourselves. Love and hate are the strongest words in our language. Love is stronger. Unfortunately, the reality is that this country is being destroyed by hate, greed, violence, and total disrespect for righteousness, truth, and justice.

We owe ourselves and future generations a better America

than we now have. It is the duty and responsibility of each and every one of us to do whatever we possibly can to stop this destructive trend of ignorance, backwardness, greed, hate, and disrespect, and help restore our honorable country to true righteousness, justice, and respectability. The worse thing in all the world is for good women and men to say nothing, do nothing, and allow these anti-American activities to continue undetested. This is our country and we can and should make it better!

The solution: Education! Education is the key to our troubles and our public schools can and must deliver! Knowing that education is and always has been a state function, it is imperative that state governments, in conjunction with local boards of education, superintendents, and especially principals and classroom teachers reverse these disruptive and destructive trends "by any means necessary."

Chapter One

Finding a Home

P hilosophically, it is said that we should rejoice and celebrate the death of a loved one and be sad, grievous, and depressed with the birth of a loved one. My experiences throughout life were the exact opposite, and I would take nothing in exchange for this incredibly inspiring and impelling journey through life's most challenging obstacle courses. Having been born May 27, 1928, in the backwoods of Fairfield County, South Carolina, and reared on a 269 acre cotton farm during a major national depression afforded me the greatest possible challenge to become whatever I wanted.

It also afforded me the greatest opportunity and justifiable reasons to say nothing, do nothing, and become nothing. The path of least resistance was followed by the vast majority of my peers. It was very easy and most popular to follow the crowd and blame something or somebody else for all of our troubles and problems. Using the adjustment mechanism known as rationalization, anything under the sun can be justified and vigorously defended.

However, I have personally made it my choice, and I hope it will be your choice, to take the high road. Become a nonconformist, take the path less traveled, and become your own unique and original person. The world is already saturated with too many carbon copy individuals. They get up each morning and check the direction the wind is blowing. Sadly, that will be the direction they will follow on that particular day. They always follow the crowd—rightly or wrongly.

We normally refer to people of this nature as having no backbone. The truth of the matter is that people who will stand for nothing will fall for anything. This nonconformist approach to life is not easy. It is not popular and in many situations it can be extremely dangerous. However, nothing in the whole world could ever be more redemptive. It represents respect, truth, honor, character, dignity, courage, commitment, perseverance, and the will and determination to succeed in whatever goals we set for ourselves.

)*()*()*()*()*()*(

At the age of five months, my mother, Mrs. Ester Boyd-Stevenson, fully aware that she was dying, gave me to Ms. Ella Stewart, the oldest of seven Stewart children. Ella was an unmarried woman with three sisters and four brothers, a mother and no father. She was one of my mother's best friends. My mother told Ella, "You will be highly successful in raising Lemmon. He will grow up to be a good boy and a great man. You will be proud of him."

My mother further stated, "I know everything will be just fine with you and Lemmon because God has shown it to me in a vision. God told me to give Lemmon to you." My mother died of Tuberculosis and complications of childbirth three weeks after my unofficial "adoption" into the Stewart family.

My adoption into the Ella Stewart family was most ironic, in view of the fact that my mother had several sisters, brothers, and several friends—all of whom were much better suited for my adoption than the Stewart family. The Stewart family, at the time of my adoption, was incredibly poor, had no formal education, and was saturated with the most dismal future possibilities. Although my mother was apparently fully aware of the reality of her decision, none of her other four children were adopted.

The Stewart family, during my early childhood, consisted of Susan, the head of the family and mother of us all; Ella Stewart, the oldest and my adopted mother; Charlie, who was married with four children, Robert, unmarried; Martha, married with two children; and Henretta, unmarried. Other family members not living in the immediate family home were Ben Stewart, who was unmarried and in the State Hospital, and Milo Stewart, who was married and living in a separate home with his wife and family.

My father, Daniel Stevenson, a widower with his four young children living with him, was also the brother of Susan Stewart. The names of his other four children were sister Nancy and brothers Walter, Robert, and Charlie. My father, who lived approximately eight miles northwest of the Stewart family, was a soldier in World War I, a farmer, and a railroad worker. He loved and supported his family as best he could. He also had two other sisters and one brother. Their names were Maggie, Laura, and Hewey. My father soon remarried a lovely lady named Lela Goins-Stevenson. She was kind to me and willing to do whatever she could to make my occasional visits pleasant and enjoyable.

The poverty stricken, uneducated cotton farming Stewart family possessed many noneconomic virtues. Outstanding among them was the family's stubborn determination to be self-sufficient, no matter how difficult the task. Susan Stewart, the head of the family and mother of us all, saw Welfare as an evil and demoralizing system that should be avoided at all costs.

Welfare, in her judgment, taught people to be "lazy, shiftless, and irresponsible."

Survival on a meekly nonproductive cotton farm during the 1930's, 40's, and 50's in Fairfield County was basically impossible. The harder we worked, the less we had. I felt that our chances for success on this farm were impossible. We were told by Susan Stewart, however, to always work hard and do our best no matter how difficult things became. "The Lord will provide." She also emphasized the importance of "being thankful for what you have and to always share what you have with others."

Fortunately, other crops were grown such as corn, wheat, oats, along with a variety of vegetables. Cotton was the major crop. Walnuts, hogs, chickens, turkeys, cattle, fruit, peanuts, and other necessary food for the family and farm animals were also produced. The land was owned by Mr. Arthur Owens. Susan Stewart and five of her children were sharecroppers on the Owens' farm. Mr. Owens was a fair, kind, and just human being who did whatever he could to help us succeed in our farm endeavors. He would always take the first two bails of cotton produced for his rent. However, if the farm produced less than three bails of cotton for the year, he would only take half of that amount.

In spite of the devastating poverty and uneducated conditions of the Stewart family, Susan Stewart was amazingly knowledgeable of and sensitive to the needs of others—especially those she perceived to be less fortunate. The best fruit, vegetables, meat, and dairy products produced by the family were given away. Susan's famous saying was, "Give to the world the best that you have and the best will come back to you." I knew many people who frequently used that famous saying, but they did not do it. They only talked about it. Susan Stewart was the only person I have ever met who actually did it. Many of the people on the receiving end, in my judgment, appeared to have much more than we had. Also, a substantially large number of those individuals were apparently lazy or, for whatever reason, refused to execute necessary work habits to produce their own food. They were constantly looking for a handout.

There was no racism in the Stewart family. We were taught to love and respect all people, work together as a team, and always support each other. Susan constantly reminded us of the "crab mentality" and she insisted that we never allow ourselves to ever behave like crabs. The story is told of about 50 crabs that found themselves trapped in a huge hole. Their only hope to safety would be to crawl out of that hole. There was a mad rush and scramble to get out of this hole. Unfortunately, every time one crab would almost crawl to the top of the hole, another crab would pull it back down into the bottom of the hole, thus the saying the "crab mentality."

Chapter Two

Beyond King Cotton and the Farm

Although my mother, father, aunts, and uncles could not read and write their names, they all possessed a type of miraculously sound and meaningful wisdom. Their will to live and survive was evident, even in spite of their deprived social, economic, and educational conditions.

"Set your mind on your goals and work on them as hard as you possibly can. You are somebody and you should be proud of yourself. God made you and God don't make junk. Never give up, never give in, and never give out no matter how hard your goals become."

The philosophy, *you can succeed if you try*, was passed on to all of us by our parents. The message of courage, commitment, determination, responsibility, and endurance came to us by word of mouth and it was repeated day after day. My sisters, brothers, and I were encouraged to pass this wisdom on to our children—nonstop "until death do we part." Some of us heard the message and used it in our lives. Others heard it not, or if they did hear it, they did not use it. Susan Stewart said on several occasions, "You can lead a horse to the water, but you cannot make him drink."

✻✻✻✻✻✻

This period in time was during a major depression for all Americans, but it was especially financially disastrous for many cotton farmers in Fairfield County. Other members of the Stewart and Stevenson families had worked in the steel mills of Baltimore, Maryland, and Harrisburg, Pennsylvania. Some of them had done very well financially. They had very nice clothes, automobiles, and money to spend.

In contrast, all of our homes in Farifield were slummy and dilapidated. King Cotton (cotton picking) had lost all of its appeal for delivering poverty stricken farmers from their misery. Therefore, farmers were beginning to look to education and industry to cure their financial woes.

The Stewart family wanted me to have a good education and they did whatever they could to help me. I was allowed to do extra work for money at the lumber mill, other farms, a barber shop, and the Fairfield Inn located in the town of Winnsboro, South Carolina. I was allowed to keep all of my earned money for my future education. When I was seven years old, my cousin Henretta would walk me six miles to the nearest black school in Shady Grove Methodist Church.

When I was eight years old, a new one-room elementary school was built one mile from my Stewart family home. I was allowed to walk alone to this school called St. John's Elementary School. Black farm children in rural South Carolina were allowed to attend school not more than six months per year. They had to help harvest crops in the fall and help plant the crops in the spring. Thus, black children were only allowed to attend school during the winter months.

Although our teachers in these one-room rural elementary schools were poorly educated, most of them were extremely dedicated. They loved their students and did whatever they could to help us learn. The teachers helped us feel worthy, as human beings, and made us work hard on the difficult tasks of learning to read, count, write, and think. Sound educational values were a part of our daily lessons. We were taught to make full use of what we had.

Teachers told us frequently, "Do not make excuses, and never allow the word *can't* to dominate your thinking and beliefs." The famous poem, *Keep a-goin* by Frank L. Stanton was constantly recited by some of my teachers.

'Taint no use to sit an' whine
When the fish ain't on your line.
Bait your hook an' keep a-tryin'-
Keep a-goin'!

I experienced a tremendous amount of difficulty learning how to read. I loved my teachers and wanted to please them anyway I possibly could. All of the students in the class had to take turns reading the lesson. Apparently, everybody in the class could read, except me. When it was time for me to read, I could not do it.

I was extremely embarrassed over my inability to read. Some of my teachers criticized me publicly as being lazy, not studying my lesson, not caring about wanting to get an education, or perhaps I was a good bit stupid. When I was called stupid before the entire class and they all laughed at me, I could not take it anymore so I asked for Ella's help.

Ella, my adopted mother, was extremely gifted and was a very intellectually brilliant woman. Although she had little or no formal education, she had miraculously learned to read, write, and think extremely well. She helped me with my reading problems every day and we worked out a solution.

We found out that I was suffering from a sight problem called astigmatism. I simply could not see the words. Knowing this was the problem, I was forced to rely on my memory. Therefore, I asked Ella to read the entire lesson to me at least two times. In order to avoid further embarrassment in the classroom, I memorized the entire reading lesson each day as Ella read it to me.

When my time came to read, I was happy and excited because my reading sounded better than any of the other students. I had memorized a lesson so well that I could read it with the book upside down. I was praised by my teacher and classmates. They never found out the real truth about my improved reading ability. Ella helped me learn most of my number facts and all of my multiplication tables. In fact, she helped me build the foundation necessary for my future education in grades five through eight.

Chapter Three

Nothing Is Impossible

I don't like the word *can't*. It almost invariably creates a **dare** in me. It forces me to surface the influence of my military training, the importance of perseverance which I learned while at South Carolina State College, and my University of Missouri training and preparedness. When that happens I become fearless, courageous and intensely fearful of the possibility of dying before having done everything I can to help provide essential, meaningful service to my fellow man and making this world a better place in which to live. Life's major obstacles are blessings and we should be proud of them because they suggest to us that maybe there are no truly great men and women. Instead, there are grave and insurmountable circumstances in which ordinary men and women like you and me are forced to meet.

※※※※※※

Compulsory education, in which children were required to attend school regularly, was nonexistent in Fairfield County. In fact, the only schooling available to rural black children was grades one through six. Any schooling beyond sixth grade had to be secured by applying to the Fairfield County Training School, located in Winnsboro. If accepted, a special fee was required for non-city resident students.

Fairfield County Training School included grades one through eleven. After completing the sixth grade at St. John's Elementary School, located at Adger, South Carolina, I established residency in Winnsboro by moving into the home of my cousin, Robert Davis. It was cheaper to pay room and board to my cousin than to pay the expensive nonresidence fee. Also, Winnsboro was approximately ten miles from the Stewart Farm, where there existed a busy, major highway. The situation created a safety hazard for me, and in addition, it was much too far to walk alone.

I can think of nothing in the totality of experiences that was more devastating, humiliating, and embarrassing than my first day at the Winnsboro Fairfield County Training School. My country farm shoes and clothes were uniquely different and inferior to those of all other students in the school. All of my seventh grade classmates wore the prettiest and best looking clothes I had ever seen. Surprisingly, they were all very receptive, kind, understanding, and helpful to me.

The teacher and students did whatever they could to help me feel welcome and truly accepted as a member of the class. My being different apparently did not matter to them. No one laughed or made fun of me, as I felt they would surely do. Unfortunately, all of my clothes were new. They were purchased for me by me with my own money. However, I bought the country fashions instead of the city fashions and could blame only myself for the mistake. I knew absolutely nothing about the city.

All of the teachers in the school appeared to be highly educated, refined, dedicated, dignified, good looking, and fully committed to insuring the academic success of the students. I could not help but be grateful, happy, and excited in such a joyous atmosphere. I was especially excited to have Ms. Nickpee as my seventh grade teacher. We all thought she was the nicest and most beautiful teacher we had ever seen. Some of us had discussed the possibility of failing seventh grade in order to remain in her class one more year. That could not happen because there were four sections of seventh grade. All retained students would be assigned to a different teacher.

Our infatuating love affair with Ms. Nickpee was disappointingly short-lived. At midyear, she got married and resigned her teaching position with the school. We wished her well and hoped for another teacher just like her. That did not happen. Our new teacher, who was well educated and highly qualified, was a major disappointment to many of us. She was much older, less beautiful, most inconsiderate, and at times, very hostile. She accepted no excuses from anyone. Superior academic performance was demanded of everyone with no exceptions tolerated. Many of us disliked her so much that we named her *Witch*.

School was becoming more and more of a bore to me and I had given serious thought to dropping out and getting a full-time job until this unpopular teacher stated to me and several other students, "Lemmon and many others of you are very nice boys, but you cannot succeed academically. I do not see a bright and successful future for you."

Her public denouncement of me and several of my friends generated enough hatred in me to reconstruct my entire outlook on school, teachers, and my future inspiration to remain in school. Hate is not all bad. I had to learn how to hate ignorance, backwardness, poverty, bigotry, social classicism, and discrimination to the degree necessary for me to pay the supreme price for their destruction. I declared war on all six above evils and injustices.

Following several depressing days and solid support from my family, friends, and other teachers in the school, I decided to make this despised teacher out to be the biggest liar in the world. I decided to finish high school, finish college, and become the type of teacher all boys and girls needed and deserved. In reality, I consider my teacher's attitude as one of the greatest blessings I have ever received. It taught me to show disrespect and total contempt for the word *can't*.

One of the most devastating and truly hostile attacks ever leveled against ignorance occurred at the Fairfield County Training School grades nine, ten, and eleven, by a three teacher team of warriors during the 40's. The team of professors consisted of Mr. Harry Boulware, for math; Mrs. Helen Belton, for science; and Mr. W.A. Ross, Sr., for English. They saturated all of us with every skill and technique we would ever need for college success. Although they possessed limited education, limited financial support and meek facilities, the teachers nevertheless guaranteed student mastery of the required skills.

Mr. Boulware, the most brilliant, understanding, flamboyant, and innovative teacher I have ever met, taught us to understand, appreciate, and love math. He also taught us to understand the relationship among general math, algebra, and geometry. He stated that math was easy and that he guaranteed that everyone of us would earn a passing grade. His common saying was, "Dag wan'it, before you leave my class, you will have learned everything in math you will need for success in college. Since you are all guaranteed a passing grade, there is never a need to worry about failing. Only think about how much fun you will have learning this stuff." He said that algebra, geometry, and all other kinds of math were simply addition, subtraction, multiplication, and division. "You learned how to do that in the seventh grade."

Although hundreds of students attended his classes, I have

never met or heard of any student who failed math, or who did not love Professor Boulware. To us, he was truly the most popular and loved teacher in all the world. He stated on one occasion that grades were dumb, backwards, stupid, and totally unnecessary. He said that our knowledge of how to solve math problems was much more important than whether we received a grade of F, D, C, B, or A.

He also told us that after working with thousands of students during his teaching career, he had never met a dumb or stupid student. "You are all smart enough to learn anything in the school you want to learn. Of course, some of you may require more time." He said that, "Five plus four equals nine, base ten. Some students may learn this fact in two minutes. Others may require several hours. Some may even require several months. The important thing is learning and being able to demonstrate mastery of the fact. No one gives a dag'onit how much learning time was required."

Every individual is uniquely different, according to Professor Boulware. Some students have mental capacities equal to a pint, a quart, or a gallon. He would say, "The pint individual can learn anything the gallon individual learns. The only difference is that the pint individual may require a little more time." Mr. Boulware's most memorable analogy was three people leaving Winnsboro at the same time, on a 20 mile race trip to Columbia, South Carolina. One was riding a bicycle, the other a motorscooter, and the third a Cadillac race car. Who should get to Columbia first? The obvious answer, according to Professor Boulvare, is the race car driver. However, they all did get to Columbia.

Mrs. Helen Belton, a science wizard and, in our judgment, truly the most beautiful human in all the world, required mastery of her science lessons. We were required to read and study each lesson, listen to her explanations of the lessons, and be able to answer correctly at least 75% of all questions she would give us on an examination. She did use grades. Many of her students received the D grade, including me.

On one occasion, she stated to me that, "When you go to college, you will take science and you will do very well." I asked her if she was aware that I had received the grade D on my science test. She said, "Of course I know you got a D, I issued the grade."

I wanted to know how I was going to succeed in college with D grades when all of the other students around me earned an A or B on their examinations. She explained that an A or a B the other students received were the only honors and glory they would ever receive. "You are going to college, you will finish college, and you will enjoy many honors during your lifetime."

Professor W.A. Ross, Sr., the school's principal, teacher of all high school basic subjects, the secretary, and when necessary, the custodian, did whatever was necessary to ensure the efficient and effective operation of the Fairfield County Training School. He had served as the principal of the school for more than 40 years and was considered by his colleagues, politicians, citizens, and former students as the most honorable, effective, and respected educator in the State of South Carolina.

Professor Ross's primary subject, during this point in time, was English/Grammar. Grammar was difficult and it caused some problems for more than 90% of the class. Professor Ross, however, made learning in all of the classes he taught easy and fun. He may have used grades, but I do not recall ever receiving a grade in his classes. He spent several extra hours working with my friend, Robert Craig, and me on the verb "to be," the difference between shall and will, and subject/verb agreement.

He also required each one of his students to demonstrate mastery of the lessons. We had fun in his classes conducting debates. He also allowed some of us to engage in arguments in which we could verbally attack each other, provided the words we used were found in the dictionary. Some of our vocabularies grew extensively.

All three of the above dynamic teachers taught us about national and international heroic role models. One of those heroes was Abraham Lincoln, the 16th president of the United States, and the great emancipator. He said that a house divided against itself cannot stand. "I believe that this government cannot endure permanently half slave and half free."

With malice toward none and charity for all, he preserved the union and freed the slaves. He declared that all men are created equal. Lincoln also said that, "There is no reason in the world why the Negro is not entitled to all of the natural rights enumerated in the Declaration of Independence—the right to life, liberty, and the pursuit of happiness. The Negro also has the right to eat the bread, without the leave of anybody else, which his own hand earns, he is my equal and the equal of every living man." All of Lincoln's major accomplishments occurred in the face of imminent danger.

We are reminded of George Washington Carver, who, born a Negro slave, among other things, won worldwide fame for his scientific experiments with peanuts and sweet potatoes. He dealt a crippling blow to King Cotton when he made more than 500 different products from peanuts and sweet potatoes. Some of the products made from the peanut included soup, coffee, ink, dyes, cheese, milk, flour, and wood stain.

His sweet potato products included rubber, vinegar, molasses, and flour. Farmers were convinced that they could make money on crops other than cotton. Also, peanuts and potatoes were good for the land. They replenished the soil while cotton depleted it. Dr. Carver said, "Measure me not by the height to which I have climbed, but the depths from which I have come." Dr. Carver used his entire life savings of $33,000 to establish the Carver Foundation.

Another role model included Booker T. Washington, born and reared a Negro slave, who, out of concern for the future welfare of his masters, cried when he was set free. He stated that he knew how to survive. He felt that his masters did not know how to survive because everything had been done for them in the past. Now, they would have to fend for themselves.

After working his way through school, Booker T. Washington became the greatest humanitarian, politician, businessman, educator, and the most effective developer the world has ever known. Washington accomplished what was considered indisputably impossible for a (former) Negro slave—he worked his way through school and established the Tuskegee Institute. The school started with 30 students in an old church. When he died in 1915, the school had developed into a faculty of 255, more than 100 buildings, and a student body of more than 3,000.

When my wife and I visited the campus of Tuskegee Institute in October 1994, we were presented with documentation confirming a faculty of 264 teachers and 98 buildings and more than 4,000 students. Also, during World War II, the school produced the best core of Air Force flyers of any other school or army worldwide. Prior to the Tuskegee flyers, the United States Air Force was losing 65 out of every 200 bombers or a total of one out of every three bombers. Tuskegee flyers escorted more than 50 bombing missions and did not lose a single bomber to enemy actions.

Most importantly, they told us about Jesus Christ, the despised one, the troublemaker, the nonconformist who proclaimed that all things are possible, if you only believe. His message that we must become doers as well as believers was clear, precise, and profound. We must hear the message, believe it, and then put it into practice. Jesus was a man of action. He was a doer and the founder of Christianity.

Although He was killed by His enemies and hypocritical friends more than 19 centuries ago, His message of love your enemies, pray for your persecutors, visit the sick, feed the hungry, and clothe the naked, is still coming through louder, clearer, and more profoundly than ever before. Even though He had no money, enjoyed no great fame, was rejected by His friends, neighbors, and community, He is still the most fascinating central figure of the human race.

Chapter Four

The Road to Self-Sufficiency

P ertaining to self-sufficiency, your mother may do for you, your father may do for you, your teacher may do for you, and your minister may do for you, but God continues to bless the child who does for himself. Also, the slogan, "Root little pig or die poor," has real meaning to most farm people. Its truism and intensive wisdom is rooted in the precious worth of work.

My role models, including teachers, ministers, counselors, and parents have constantly stated that individuals who do not work should not eat. Work builds character, generates thriftiness, pride, instills self-worth and most importantly, it enables the individual to provide essential services to his fellow man—especially those less fortunate.

High on the list of services should be young people who have not had the chance to grow up, develop, and assume full responsibility for their existence. Also, there is another major benefit to work and other invigorating physical activities. It makes and keeps you physically fit—especially farm work. There is no known substitute for exercise and physical fitness. Although I did not appreciate it at the time, having to walk six miles per day to school was a healthy blessing. I felt good and

I do not ever recall being sick during my elementary and high school years.

)()()()()()(

I learned at an early age the value and love of money and that perhaps the only way I would ever get money would be to work and save what I earned. My room and board were free. I do not recall ever hating work, but I have hated working for nothing. I wanted to get paid well for my work. When I was nine years old, I worked three days a week for Mr. Hickson at 50 cents per day. I went to school the other two days. I saved all of my earnings.

When I was ten years old, I continued my three days per weeks' work with the Hickson's, but I also worked Saturdays for Mr. Hicklon, the other farmer west of the Stewart farm. At first, Mr. Hicklon paid me 50 cents per day, but he later changed it to 75 cents per day. At that point, I stopped working for Mr. Hickson and worked for Mr. Hicklon four days per week or whenever he needed me. Although I was not well paid for my work, it was regular and I learned how to save every dime of my earnings for college.

My next areas of employment included five days per week at the Fairfield Inn and one day per week at the Mack McKocker's barber shop. I was twelve years old. My earnings were approximately 25 cents per hour at the Fairfield Inn and approximately $1.25 per hour at the barber shop. My initial salary at the barber shop was 40% of my total earnings. Haircuts were 50 cents. The average time required per customer was about eight to ten minutes.

At the age of fourteen, I was fired from the Fairfield Inn. I continued my work at the barber shop and got a five day per week job at the lumber mill, which was located at Adger, South

Carolina. My salary was approximately 35 to 50 cents per hour. Having been licensed as a registered barber for the state of South Carolina, my barber shop earnings had increased to 60% of every dollar earned.

At the age of 19, I had saved approximately $3,500 for the purpose of buying four years of college training at any college or university that would accept me. I had a major interest in Virginia State College, located in Petersburg, VA; Fisk University, located in Nashville, TN; and Tuskegee Institute located in Tuskegee, AL. Several months before I planned to enter college, a tragedy struck the family. Mr. Arthur Owens, the owner of the 269 acre farm, died.

The farm was willed to his three children. However, he had arranged with them, before he died, to at least allow the Stewart family the opportunity to purchase the farm before it was ever put on the market for sale. His heirs were kind enough to at least notify us that the farm would be put up for sale. They stated that, "Our father wanted you to have every possible opportunity to purchase this property. Therefore, we will allow you three months to secure the required funds for its purchase."

The initial asking price was $6,000. The actual selling price, however, was $2,750 after the Owens family arranged to cut and sell available farm timber. The Stewart family had no money, no credit, and absolutely no possibility of ever securing the necessary funds to purchase the farm. The reality was that the land would definitely be sold and the Stewart family would be homeless. Henretta had approximately $250, I had approximately $3,500, and all other individual household members had nothing. I needed every dime I had and could possibly earn within the next four or five years to pay for my college education. I wanted to go to college more than anything in the world.

Susan Stewart's son, Milo Stewart, who lived in a separate

home, was a railroad worker and was believed to have had sufficient funds to purchase the property. Susan and Robert approached Milo to request that he either purchase the property and own it outright or loan the necessary funds to them. Milo refused on both counts. He would not loan Susan the money because she and her family had absolutely no means by which to repay him. He did not want to purchase the land for himself. He also stated that he had to purchase a car for his sons. He implied that he would not be able to live with his family if he did not purchase the automobile.

Robert Stewart came to me on three different occasions, asking me to use my college money to purchase the place. I refused. During his third request to me, he stated that if I would put up the money, there is no way the family would let me "fall" in college. He had been drinking on that particular day, and I became very angry with him for harassing me about my college money. I told him that I was not responsible for the family having no money, there was no way in the world he or anybody else in the family could ever pay my college expenses, and we argued.

Susan Stewart heard the conflict and arranged a meeting in which Robert, Ella, Henretta, and I attended. She stated, among other things, "Rob, that is Lemmon's money. He has earned every penny of it honestly. If he does not want to put his money in the farm, he does not have to. I glory in his spunk. I wish him well in college. I am not worried about myself and this family. The Lord will provide. He has always taken care of us. He is taking care of us now, and He will always take care of us."

I was bitterly opposed to giving up my college money because I had to get away from that farm. The farm was, to me, a type of prison where you worked from sun up to sun down. In fact, I considered the farm cruel and unusual punishment.

However, I was so moved by Susan Stewart's comments that I met with the same group, put up the $3,000 needed, and started making other arrangements to attend college.

Specifically, a non-written verbal agreement was made among Robert Stewart, Henretta Stewart, Susan Stewart, Ella Stewart, and me. The content of the agreement was that the land would not be mortgaged, it would not be sold, it would not be given away, and in the end, it would belong to me. The land would provide lifetime food and shelter for all initial family members and after their deaths, everything would be passed on to me.

Everyone agreed, initially, that the land should be placed in Susan Stewart's name. Susan objected. She stated that she was too old. It was later decided that the land would be placed in the names of the two youngest, fully adult members of the family. The land did not belong to them. They would simply act as guardians. I was considered a child and the agreed upon names were Robert and Henretta. It was felt that two names on the deed were better than one name only. In this way, one could prevent the other from doing something foolish or betray the trust of the family agreement.

We were, at all times, totally ignorant of the law. This was a strong unwritten family pact. I have always felt of it as an unfaltering trust or a perfect reliance binding on the immediate family members. I now understand that the legal name for this agreement is Resulting Trust. No one in our family had ever made or executed a will, because we had never had anything to will. Also, no one in the history of the Stewart and Stevenson families has ever owned or inherited any land.

Further, we all felt it would be humanly impossible for anyone even remotely connected to our family to conspire with an attorney or anyone else to deprive us of the land. There had always been simply too much pride, self-respect, and family honor to ever try to "get or take something for nothing." We were, and always had been, a self-sufficient family. It simply never occurred to us that younger generations of the family or family in-laws would ever be so selfish, greedy, dishonest, and evil to the degree necessary to try to destroy what the family had developed and maintained during the past 48 years.

Even though I put up the initial money for purchasing the farm, Henretta Stewart, the only other money earning member of the initial family who worked around the clock, day and night, put all of her earnings into taxes, major repairs, and upkeep of the property. As of June 1994, she was 80 years old and one of the remaining living initial family member who knows the full details of what occurred during the purchase of the property. She was involved in all meetings, planning, and other farm business activities and is one of the living bona fide witnesses to what happened.

I am convinced, beyond a reasonable doubt, that if I had not put up the money for the farm and the family secured it some other way, the immediate family would have still passed it on to me. The goal was to control the farm situation in such a manner that it would be there to serve and benefit the members of the then current members of the home. No thought or concern was ever given to heirs or future generations of the family. As of 1997, Henretta and I are the only two remaining members of the immediate 1947 Stewart-Stevenson family household.

Susan Stewart, a widow and head of a large household for more than 20 years before I was born, knew, as few people did, how ruthless and totally destructive racist hate groups could be. Minority women and particularly Negro women with large families were especially vulnerable to evil white supremacy attacks. Accordingly, Susan, who had been blessed with unlimited divine wisdom, counseled every member of the family about the probable danger we faced.

We were all gravely concerned that some evil, vicious, selfish, jealous, fee-greedy attorney or some other legal genius might conspire with one or more of the racist hate groups located in the state and literally drive us from our home. Because of this concern, we all agreed that we would never discuss the property situation and hopefully no one, outside of our immediate family, would ever know or find out that we were property owners. This 269 acre farm was centered around property owned by whites, many of whom would have gladly given anything to own our land.

Mr. Owens and his family, fully aware of the risk and possible hardships facing the family, made absolutely certain no information got out pertaining to the selling of the plantation. It was always, day-after-day and year-after-year, business as usual. There was a bond existing between Susan Stewart and Arthur Owens that was far superior to anything I have ever heard or seen.

Susan convinced Mr. Owens that she and her family would willingly and gladly, with no strings attached, produce more cotton or any other crop of his choice, than any other family or groups of families anywhere in the world. Mr. Owens, a humanitarian, who loved justice, mercy, and righteousness, and who hated all forms of evil and human suffering, provided Susan with solid unwavering support and defense. I have always respected, admired, and wanted to be just like the man.

Chapter Five

First Mountaintop

*T*he honorable Dr. Martin Luther King, Jr., spoke most eloquently about God's allowing him to go up on the mountaintop. I have experienced the good fortune of going up on several mountaintops during my lifetime. The first one includes that glorious day in the fall of 1948 when I was finally accepted as a regular student in South Carolina State College's Freshman Class. I was very warmly received by several important professors at the college, including the president.

Circumstances and conditions leading up to this honor had been most disappointing. I no longer had the use of several thousand dollars I had religiously saved for my college education, and I simply could not understand, at that time, how I could ever attend college without money. Although I did not give up or completely quit, I was seriously depressed and began to wonder if I really had what it took to face a four-year college environment and succeed.

I felt somewhat like Moses when he said: Why me? Surely you can find somebody else who would be better suited for this mission. I have just left Egypt. I know what Pharaoh is like, and I cannot handle it. That's why I left in the first place.

This paraphrasing of Moses is how I felt. My self-esteem

had obviously hit an all time low. I reviewed all of the literature I could find concerning my role models and also introduced myself to another poem entitled, *A Psalm of Life* by Longfellow. It was very motivating and uplifting for me. The part I like best was:

> *In the bivouac of life, Be not like dumb, driven cattle! Be a hero in the strife! . . . Let us then be up and doing. With a heart for any fate; Still achieving, still pursuing, Learn to labor and to wait . . . Lives of great men all remind us We can make our lives sublime, And, departing, leave behind us, Footprints on the sands of time.*

I also read and studied *Invictus* by William Ernest Henley. The impressive part of that poem for me included:

> *It matters not how straight the gate, How charged with punishments the scroll, I am the master of my fate; I am the captain of my soul.*

I also read, very extensively, parts of the Bible, including Proverbs, the Prophet Isaiah, and the Book of Psalms. At this point, I was determined to do what had to be done which was to forget my troubles of the past and move on to more challenging experiences of the future. When Mrs. Helen Belton found out that I had spent all of my college money to prevent the Stewart family from becoming homeless, she told me that I did the only right thing there was to do. She said that if I had walked out on the Stewarts during their crisis, I would have never been able to live with myself.

She also said, "Lemmon, that is your home, as well as a place for the family to live. You do not have to worry one minute about going to college. It will not be easy and you may not be able to attend the college of your choice, but I guarantee that you will go to college."

Mrs. Belton introduced me to the poem *If* by Rudyard Kipling (1865-1936) which said, in part:

> *If you can keep your head when all about you*
> *Are losing theirs and blaming it on you,*
> *If you can trust yourself when all men doubt you,*
> *But make allowance for their doubting too.*
> *If you can wait and not be tired by waiting,*
> *Or, being lied about, don't deal in lies,*
> *Or being hated don't give way to hating . . .*
> *If you can bear to hear the truth you've spoken*
> *Twisted by knaves to make a trap for fools,*
> *Or watch the things you gave your life to, broken,*
> *And stooped and build 'em up with worn-out tools.*
> *If you can make one heap of all your winnings*
> *And risk it on one turn of pitch-and-toss,*
> *And lose, and start again at your beginnings,*
> *And never breathe a word about your loss: . . .*
> *And so hold on when there is nothing in you*
> *Except the Will which says to them: "Hold on!" . .*
> *And if you can fill the unforgiving minute*
> *With sixty seconds' worth of distance run.*
> *Yours is the Earth and everything that's in it,*
> *And - which is more - you'll be a Man, my son!*

One week later, she told her husband, Mr. David Belton, "David, take Lemmon to South Carolina State College. I have talked with him and I know his circumstances. There is no way in the world he can make out an application to any college in this country and be accepted. It just won't happen. He doesn't have enough required money to get accepted. Take him in the back door, and talk to the food service manager. If the food manager won't help, go directly to Mother Wilkinson. I know she will help."

I got my room and board free, through the help of Mr. and Mrs. David Belton. During the Summer of 1947, I got a full-time six-days-a-week job as a registered barber in the city of Baltimore, Maryland. I was paid 65% of every dollar earned. Haircuts cost approximately $2.00. I made the necessary money for my first year of college. The following year, I was the college barber in which I cut students, professors, and other staff members hair. I also earned room and board by working in the college dining room at South Carolina State College, located in Orangeburg, South Carolina.

At this point in time, I was already a highly skilled, fast, and extremely lucky registered barber. I had many more customers than I could handle. I charged 50 cents per haircut. All of my professors and student customers voluntarily paid me $1.50 to $2.00 per job. When my work backed up, some of the students would set up study sessions in my college room. In this way, some of the students would read and discuss the lesson while I cut hair. I was earning money from haircuts and being prepared for my daily college classes at the same time. Goethe's Faust is an example of one such lesson.

Even with all the time in the world, I would have had difficulty reading and understanding that literature lesson. Several of my classmates discovered a comic book containing this story. It was very easy to read and fully understand. Also, several honorable professors told me that the only thing I needed to do was to maintain an open mind, decide as specifically and precisely as possible what it was that I wished the college to help me accomplish, and be willing to work continuously and as hard as possible on my goals.

In so many words, the professors stated: You can succeed no matter how difficult your circumstances may have been. Think in the present. Do not waste time thinking about the past. You are at South Carolina State College now, and we have nothing in the world more important to do than to see to it that you get all the help, assistance, and assurance you will ever need for success. Helping students is our job and we are good at it.

Following this honorable, heartwarming reception given to me by the majority of faculty members, I began to perceive that dying and going to heaven could not possibly be much greater than this. I was determined not to let those honorable people down. I was determined never to disappoint them. Although my reading skills were limited and it was necessary for me to work my way through school, I constantly used whatever available time I had to read anything I could get my hands on. I learned to love and appreciate the library better than any other place in the world.

My decision to major in agriculture came following several conferences with state and county farm agents when it was clear to me that the best opportunities for employment and also the highest salaries were paid to professional teachers of agriculture. Most importantly, the majority of agriculture teachers in the State of South Carolina, during that period of time, were principals of their schools. Agriculture teachers were employed for 12 months and they were, by far, the most respected professional people in their communities.

They were extremely well trained because they had to take all required educational courses of other regular teachers, along with several additional technical and scientific agriculture courses. The agriculture teachers had to teach science, math, and other regular classes, along with being able to demonstrate meaningful techniques of farming skills such as cattle, swine, vegetables, and poultry, and knowledge of grains such as wheat, oats, barley, corn, cotton, and other farm crops. The successful and effective agriculture teacher had to be a shrewd business person, guidance counselor, politician, and highly skilled in working with other people, especially those less fortunate. Agriculture teachers and county farm agents had lovely homes, beautiful automobiles, and the finest and most beautiful clothes money could buy.

It would be most unrealistic and totally dishonest if I did not state, in spite of all the love, assurance, and solid support of South Carolina State College faculty, my profound infatuation with what many people would call the nigger mentality. Examples of this mentality include, but by no means are limited to: (1) My cup is half empty instead of my cup is half full. (2) They really do not care about me. They are only trying to be polite. (3) She does not want me in her class, and I will definitely receive a failing grade, no matter what I do! (4) My high school was not accredited by the state of South Carolina and, therefore, State College will not let me become a regular State College student. (5) They are Uncle Toms who have been programmed by the white man. (6) You definitely cannot trust those people because they will only be nice to you until they gain your confidence. They will then destroy you as soon as they possibly can. (7) They don't want me down here because I am poor and my parents are not teachers or preachers.

In other words, I found myself constantly looking for justifiable reasons to wallow in my own self-pity. This nigger mentality, as used in this particular situation, refers to anything that is dirty, backward, dumb, stupid, foolish, outrageously negative and totally depletes or destroys self-esteem. Such a person is also scared and is a complete indisputable coward. He is complacent and always blaming something or somebody else for all of his problems.

Any human, regardless of race, gender, or nationality, can be a nigger or be saturated with the nigger mentality. Under no circumstances is the word nigger to be confused with the word Negro, which refers to a human being of color.

I am eternally grateful to one South Carolina State College

professor who single-handedly derailed me of my overt nigger mentality in one 35 minutes conference. I had expressed to several State College teachers that I was extremely deficient in test taking skills. I could not read well and my math skills were deficient. One of these teachers suggested that I make an appointment to talk with a psychology professor known as Howard Jordan. He had supposedly helped hundreds of students overcome their lack of self-confidence.

Dr. Jordan started the conference by reminding me of a common public domain statement that said: He who knows not and knows not that he knows not, he is simple, teach him. He who knows and knows that he knows is wise, follow him. He who knows not and does not know that he knows not, he is a fool and you should get and stay as far away from him as you possibly can!

He further stated, "Lemmon, you have apparently diagnosed your case carefully. You know what you want to do and you know your strengths and weaknesses. Our immediate goal should be to build upon your strength. One of your obvious strengths is a desire and total commitment to getting a good education. We can definitely be helpful to you in this effort."

I interrupted Dr. Jordan with a score of reasons why my cause was a lost one. I felt that I did not, in fact, have enough strength to overcome my incredible weaknesses. Every positive idea offered to me by Dr. Jordan was shot down by a negative from me. Dr. Jordan finally said, "All right then, Mr. Stevenson, I finally get the message. Maybe we are fighting a losing battle. You just may not have what it takes to be a real South Carolina State College man. A man who knows where he wants to go and who is willing to pay any price and bear any burden to reach his goal. Maybe the State College faculty and I should not be wasting our time with a 'Can't do individual like yourself.' Even though you definitely have unlimited possibilities, you have obviously chosen to follow the negative something-for-nothing path. I would strongly urge you to find some other institution. South Carolina State College does not have time or space for losers. Mr. Stevenson, should you ever change your mind and decide to be a winner, you know where to find me."

Dr. Jordan also left behind a short poem entitled, *Be the Best*. I had heard the poem read by my teachers before and thought it was a public domain document with an unknown author. I now understand the person who wrote the poem was Douglas Mallock. It goes like this:

If you can't be a pine on the top of a hill, be a shrub in the valley . . . but be the best little shrub by the side of the hill, be a bush if you can't be a tree. If you can't be a highway, just be a trail. If you can't be the sun, be a star; it isn't by size that you win or fail—be the best of whatever you are.

I never had another conference with Dr. Jordan and I never had the opportunity to take a course under him. However, he unmistakably got his message across to me. After several day's reflections on what Dr. Jordan and other professors had said to me, I concluded that South Carolina State College was my home and it would take the Devil and all of his Angels working full-time, until Hell freezes over, to get me out of South Carolina State College before graduation. I actually earned a Bachelors and Masters Degree from South Carolina State College, the home of true, solid, and indisputable winners.

South Carolina State College, which was established in 1896 from the Morrill Land-Grant Act of 1862, represented the one and only equality of educational opportunity for South Carolina's black people. Thomas E. Miller, the college's first president, is credited with making State College equal to any other college where blacks could be educated. President Miller F. Whittaker, the honorable, courageous, and most daring college president of all times, had another idea. He was not interested in South Carolina State College being only equal to other colleges, he was determined to make it better than other colleges or one of the best colleges anywhere in the world.

It was my good fortune to have the opportunity to meet and talk with President Whittaker during my freshman year. He was truly "Mr. Refinement." He immediately became the most influential role model I have ever experienced. I wanted to be just like him. He and his highly efficient, dedicated, and totally committed teaching staff told me to forget all of the enthusiasm and excitement I had for wanting to attend Virginia State College, Fisk University, and the Tuskegee Institute. His legacy, in his own words, is still speaking to me.

"I have an idea for this college. It is this: That each student shall give evidence of high moral character and personal worth, serious intellectual effort, and an understanding of his obligation to society. Things of the spirit, the common virtues of courtesy, honesty, integrity, and tolerance are just as important as the training of the intellect. To this end we would have this college print an indelible stamp of culture and refinement on its students. I would not have them become snobbish, but I would have them exhibit to the world by their manner of behavior and speech—there goes a State College man or State College woman."

The significance of South Carolina State College is the fact that it has provided quality educational opportunities to thousands of individuals from South Carolina and other states in the nation and the world for more than one hundred years. It is integrated, and it has amazingly met the academic standards and requirements necessary for true university status.

Chapter Six

All Things Come to an End

I t has been said and I agree that there are at least two certainties that at one time or another will confront all of us. Those certainties are change and death. The ability to understand and survive change is our major concern. Individuals who learn how to adjust to change will not have to worry about other life problems, including death. The primary lesson we must all learn is how to go with the flow. Yesterday is gone and tomorrow is not promised. However, we do have today. If we will make necessary adjustments to the changes of today, we will not have to worry about tomorrow.

)()()()()(

In spite of all the pride, love, honor, and glory President Whittaker brought to South Carolina State College and its family of teachers and students, along with his apparent youthful and inexhaustible energetic look, he died in 1949. The new president, Dr. Benny C. Turner, vowed to carry on President Whittaker's great works.

After going through that incredible adjustment period as a South Carolina State College freshman student and learning how to stop making excuses and truly compete, unconditionally, with other students at the college, my four year college term was over. I became an official graduate from South Carolina State College on June 2, 1952. College had become the most exciting and enjoyable part of my life, and I definitely did not want to leave. I finally realized that I never had it so good.

Now the thought of going back to that cotton farm offered little or no excitement for me. Also, and perhaps most importantly, I had to continue earning enough money to help defray the cost of basic upkeep of the farm. The farm income was so incredibly low that there was never enough money to pay taxes and maintain minimum living quarters.

The span of time between June 2, 1952, when I graduated from South Carolina State College, and April 1965, when I was recruited as principal of Joseph E. Beck Junior Senior High School, in Greenville, South Carolina, includes many inspiring, aggressive, and profoundly challenging assignments. Outstanding among those adventurous assignments include marriage, building and establishing a new dream home, serving as high school agriculture and science teacher, serving two years in the United States Army in which 18 months were spent in Europe, serving as teacher and principal of an elementary school which included Grades 1 through 8, spending several summers and one full year as a graduate student at the University of Missouri, and occupying a three year principalship of a senior high school which included Grades 1 through 12.

Having longed for a truly nice home and a new automobile, I decided to get married and establish a second separate home. Our newly constructed dream home was located in the most prestigious Negro section in the City of Winnsboro. It was about eight miles from my original farm home. I employed a professional lumber jack to cut, according to specifications, all of the lumber needed to build our dream home. The lumber was cut from the farm I had purchased with my college money. My brother-in-law, Mr. Mansel Ross, was a professional builder and also a brick mason. He built for my wife and me one of the most gorgeous homes ever constructed in the City of Winnsboro.

To go with this dream home, we purchased a new 1956 Mercury which was better known as the "Big M." Although we were flat broke and had incurred considerable debt, I was so pleased with our situation that I considered it my second mountaintop.

At this particular point in time, I had served as agriculture and science teacher at Finley Senior High School in Chester, South Carolina, for three months, served 18 months in the United States Army, which included one year in France and was, as of 1955, Principal of Mitford School. The school included grades 1 through 8. My wife was a teacher in one of the city elementary schools.

Fortunately, I was able to earn enough money to pay our basic living expenses from the barber shop. I worked with the school district Mondays through Fridays, and cut hair on Saturdays. Both of our teaching salaries were placed in a special bank account for emergency use only.

The teaching profession required continued schooling and special preparation throughout my career. I started working towards a masters degree under the G.I. Bill, which was completed in 1958. I also started working towards the doctorate degree in 1958. There was no graduate school in South

Carolina for blacks beyond the masters degree. Segregation laws prohibited blacks from attending the University of South Carolina. Although many black professionals from South Carolina attended Columbia and New York Universities, the total cost for such training was most excessive, and I did not wish to increase the family indebtedness.

I wrote to several other border and Midwestern universities and was rejected by all of them except one, the University of Missouri, which accepted me unconditionally. There was no additional cost or penalty for being a nonresident student. I was accepted and given the same guidance, reinforcement, and support any other Missouri University student received. They never promised me a rose garden, but equality of educational opportunity was definite.

My major reason for going to the University of Missouri was to get a good education. If I could earn another degree during this educational process, I would be delighted. However, I was not about to allow the desire to earn another advanced degree undermine my chances to get a good education. A good education for me meant, at that point in time, being fully prepared to function effectively as a school administrator, at any level, segregated or integrated.

It also meant preparing and conditioning other professionals for a similar mission, state and national. I had been advised that the University of Missouri was one of the best schools in the nation for all areas, except journalism. It was rated, by one of my professors who was a graduate of the University of Missouri, as the one and only best journalism schools in the world.

Following several summers of intensive graduate studies, my excitement about the University of Missouri was so profound that I wanted to receive a leave of absence from my work and spend one full year at the university. The university agreed to the year's resident study. My employers back in Winnsboro, South Carolina, did not agree.

When I approached my superintendent about the leave of absence, he was extremely nice, at first. He said, "Lemmon, I think you would want to think about this situation. You already have enough education. You have your master's degree, and you are one of the best principals in this county. You have a lovely wife and four fine children. You have a lovely brand new home and a beautiful new car. What more do you want? You were an ROTC student, served in the military, and traveled all over Europe. I simply do not think you need any more training. I want you to think about it and then come back and let me know what you decided."

I had a follow-up meeting with him several days later, and he was hostile, resentful, and nasty. He shouted, "We will never give you a leave of absence. Besides, we probably will be able to find somebody who is a whole lot better than you! If you want to go to that school, you will have to resign your position." I thanked him for the time he spent with me and walked away.

A black person resigning a sound, effective, convenient, and indisputably secure principalship during the 1960's was unthinkable. The school was new and one of the most modern, innovative plants in the county. We had a dedicated, efficient, and effective staff. Additionally, it was the only school in the county and perhaps the only school in the State of South Carolina that conducted pre and post-standardized testing for all students, grades one through eight.

The academic achievement of our students, as measured by the Stanford Achievement Test, was equal to and in several cases, superior to that of the nation. Each and every one of our students looked forward to the opportunity to take the standardized test in order to beat their past record of performance. Our students were not only in competition with other students throughout the nation, but they were in competition with themselves. This particular testing program was part of an action research project I was conducting as part of my graduate work at the University of Missouri.

I had heard many times that black students could not compete favorably with white students on standardized tests. I simply had to find out, for my own satisfaction, if there was any truth to this accusation. The first time the test was given, our students did not only perform poorly, their performance was a total disaster. Over 90% of our students did not score high enough to get on the measuring scale. Their performance could not be measured and compared with other students.

Because of my knowledge of testing in high school, college, the army, and the University of Missouri, I expected my students to score low during the first session. However, I expected their scores to improve drastically during the second testing session. I was in complete charge of the testing situation and the testing procedures were followed verbatim. The tests were kept under lock and key. One of the many complaints I received from students were that they did not have enough time. I informed them that they were given the same amount of time other students throughout the nation were given. They were expected to use the time given and not think about or expect additional time. I informed them that they were just as good and just as smart as any other humans anywhere in the world. I told them that their low scores on the test were due to the fact that they had never had the experience or opportunity of ever taking a standardized test.

The whole situation changed when we reorganized all curriculum courses and developed objective tests for each subject, such as reading, math, social studies, science, and spelling, in the standardized testing format. Teacher-made tests consisted of 75-100 objective questions instead of the usual 5-10 essay questions in which the students would receive 10 or 20 points for each question answered correctly. The teacher-made tests were much more difficult than any known standardized test. This was a conditioning process. If our students could pass the most difficult teacher-made tests, the standardized tests would be truly easy fun and games.

Several of our teachers felt that we were setting ourselves up to be fired for incompetence. My response to them was that, "If we teach, our students will learn. There is no doubt in my mind about this. I know you can teach and our project is, therefore, guaranteed to succeed. We have everything to gain and absolutely nothing to lose."

It had been said that hungry children could not learn. Many of our students could not afford the cost of a school lunch. All of the district school lunch programs were in the red, and we were feeding less than half of our students. This situation changed at the Mitford School overnight. I had the experience of observing two of our students eating out of the garbage can. At that point, I assumed full responsibility for two drastic changes. The first one was to reduce the lunch price each student paid by 50%.

The second thing was to require the staff to collect whatever they could from each student, even if it was only a penny, and make sure each child in attendance was fed each day. We actually collected more money on the first day of the new program than we had ever collected before. Within one month, our lunch program was out of the red. Our commodity program doubled because we were feeding twice as many students.

It was not how much we charged the students that made the difference, but rather how much we were able to collect. This was a farming community and many of our parents would donate vegetables to the school. We also received cash donations from anonymous sources. Several checks were written to the school from our community neighbors who stated that their only wish was that I would keep my mouth shut about the money and continue to feed and educate their children.

At this particular point in time, our students were ahead of the national average academically. The pride and self-respect in our home, school, and community was so high that we were able to create and build a float for the city of Winnsboro's Christmas parade. Our float won first place in competition with all the other schools and agencies in the city and county. The Junior Chamber of Commerce presented our school with a check of $75.00, along with a picture and newspaper article about our innovative competition with all other schools in the county. I called it miraculous. My students and teachers called it doing what comes naturally. They emphasized the fact that we have always been the most innovative school in the state, and "we know we can do anything we set our minds to and we can do it just as well, if not better than anybody else in the world."

In view of the fact that we had officially declared war on ignorance, assassinated, and honorably buried **"Mr. and Mrs. Can't,"** I felt this overwhelming and compelling need to get as much education as I possibly could and then share it with as many young people throughout the country as possible. I truly wanted to keep my job at Mitford. However, I was also committed to continuing my education at the University of Missouri. Accordingly, I submitted perhaps the shortest letter of resignation in the district's history. The letter said, "I hereby submit my letter of resignation from the Mitford School, effective immediately. Sincere thanks are extended to all who helped insure the success of Mitford School. Sincerely, Lemmon Stevenson."

One of the four professors at the University of Missouri who had been most understanding, helpful, and supportive of my candidacy as a graduate student asked if I would be attending the university during the fall session. I informed her that my request for a one year leave of absence had been denied and it would be necessary for me to resign my principalship. When she found out how much my annual salary was, she said, "You certainly have little or nothing to lose by resigning from that school. I am certain you will be able to find another job paying at least six times your current salary."

She discussed with me the possibility of getting a job in St. Louis, Missouri, and also serving as Director of Experimental Laboratory School at one of the nearby universities. She had supervised the dissertation of a college president who needed a laboratory school director. This particular college president had asked her to recommend a suitable director. She said, "I will be delighted to recommend an innovative administrator like yourself, if you are interested."

In April 1962, I received a telephone call from the principal of Elizabeth Heights School informing me that the principalship of the school was "wide open." The principal began by saying, "They need a principal and you have been recommended. They all know you from the outstanding work you did at the Mitford School. The job is definitely yours if you want it. I am leaving the state of South Carolina in order to take a principalship in the Durham, North Carolina, area."

Three days later, the superintendent of the Great Falls School District called and asked me to assume principalship of the Elizabeth Heights School immediately. Because of my profound interest in and lifelong desire to be a high school principal, I turned down the opportunity to direct a laboratory school at a university in Missouri and graciously accepted the principalship of Elizabeth Heights High School in Great Falls, South Carolina.

It was during this particular period of my growth and development that I concluded, beyond a reasonable doubt, that the school definitely existed for the child.   It has no other justifiable reason for existing other than for the total growth and development of each child into a fine and worthwhile individual in society. The school does not exist for boards of education, superintendents, principals, teachers, parents, citizens of the county, state, nation and politicians. It follows, therefore, that public school budgets are generally excessive, unrealistic, and slanted in the wrong direction.

Chapter Seven

Second Mountaintop

*L*ife is, without question, the most unpredictable phenom-
ena imaginable. No human being has ever been able to
fully understand it. Life's answer to all of our questions is
"maybe yes or maybe no." There is absolutely nothing for which
we can be certain.

When I was a college student, it was my good fortune to
meet and associate with a large number of students from
Greenville, South Carolina. Greenville's girls were the smartest and most beautiful humans of my experience. Greenville's
boys were the smartest and best dressed individuals I had ever
met. They also drove new expensive automobiles. I was completely hooked on the Greenville image.

When I graduated from college, I wrote several letters and
filed several applications for a teaching job in the Greenville
school system. The school system did not bother to respond to
any of my letters or applications. I was devastated! However,
life was "cool, calm, and collected." Symbolically, life had other
plans for Lemmon Stevenson. Life criticized and condemned
me for setting and attempting to accomplish goals that were
too small. I wanted to be a school teacher. Life wanted me to
be a school principal and also a professional educational ad-

ministrator—not only in South Carolina, but in Pennsylvania and any other state in this nation. I finally got the message!

)()()()()()(

The fact that my three year tenure at Elizabeth Heights High School produced several impossibilities, according to many State School officials, it is my belief that at least one of those state officials recommended me to the Greenville, South Carolina School District officials. It is a certainty that I received a letter from the Greenville School District stating that I had been recommended to become principal of the new innovative Beck Junior/Senior High School in Greenville. The compelling $2,000,000 school was approximately 80% complete.

The Greenville school officials had been informed that I was an outstanding school principal at Mitford and Elizabeth Heights Schools. The Greenville School Superintendent informed me that under no circumstances would I ever be told the name of the individual who recommended me. He was obviously a powerful and most influential person, because I am told that I was selected over more than 200 other applicants. I am eternally grateful to the individual or individuals responsible for that humanitarian deed, and I also trust that the responsible individual was not disappointed with my leadership performance as the first Principal of Beck School.

The Beck High School Yearbook of 1969 reveals a comprehensive, innovative, and modern grade seventh through twelfth school which is located in the most thickly populated Negro section of Greenville. The school was named in honor of Mr. Joseph E. Beck, a Negro educator who had spent 30 years in Greenville County school work. The plant consisted of 40 classrooms, a library which accommodated 120 students, a vocational shop complex, laboratories for biology, chemistry, general science, cosmetology, and home economics. The auditorium had a seating capacity of 600, with band, chorus, and art departments housed in this isolated area that did not interfere with regular class activities.

The gymnasium, which seated more than 1,500 people, was provided with an electrically operated panel that divided the area into two separate sections. The assistant principal was Mr. Albert A. Richburg, and the Dean of Guidance was Mrs. Nancy Griggs. Although the school was built to serve 1,000 students, its enrollment has constantly consisted of 1,500 to 1,600 students. The school had more than 355 graduates.

The school's student council adopted a school motto which was, Service, Simplicity, and Sincerity. The council decided upon the school's colors as black and gold, developed the annual homecoming festivities, and created charters for 16 clubs—three of which are nationally affiliated. They are the Student Council, National Honor Society, and Future Homemakers of America.

The school chorus, the 120 piece marching band, and the undefeatable Panther basketball team were among the most outstanding student organizations to be found anywhere in the world. Also, Beck had a very good South Carolina AAA Conference football team. Its track and baseball teams were outstanding.

In addition to the basic courses of reading, English, math, science, and social studies, Beck offered band, auto mechanics, masonry, industrial arts, trigonometry, shorthand, comparative government, advanced typing, advanced cosmetology, health education, Spanish, business math, economics, and journalism. Driver education, office practice, speech, sociology, string music, and advanced French and Spanish were also offered.

More than two-thirds of Beck's students came from families earning less than $2,000 per year, therefore it was classified as a Title I school. Accordingly, Beck has always endeavored to improve the quality and quantity of educational opportunities available for its students. The school was fully accredited by the State of South Carolina in one year. However, Beck was determined to be among the best high schools in the world, and it was fully accredited by the Southern Association of Colleges and Schools in December 1968. This project, which normally takes eight to ten years was completed in two and one-half years.

Preferring to achieve integration on a voluntary basis, the Beck staff integrated the school by employing eleven white teachers. This achievement was the outstanding one in the integration of school faculties in the State of South Carolina.

Beck's history is relatively short, having experienced only four years of operation, but the advances the school made in its educational program and in the programs of the district and the state in such a short time were remarkable. If past performance and efforts can be continued within the school and be coupled by full administrative and financial support from the School District of Greenville County, Joseph E. Beck High School will become the most outstanding high school in South Carolina.

In 1969, Beck was honored with one of the most dynamic, aggressive, dedicated, effective, and courageous 56 member teaching and administrative staff the world has ever known. It was 20% integrated and our eight member social studies staff was 50% white. Without that solid staff, district, supervisory, and community support, Beck would have had no chance of ever becoming exemplary.

Our Beck High School mission was clear, precise, and saturated with an undeniable and compelling drive to "delivering the best possible educational and support services to the black

community group farthest down on the ladder of respectability, acceptance, and honor." It was imperative that we instill
into the hearts and minds of each Beck student the invaluable
importance of hard work, responsibility, dignity, pride, respect
for the rights of others, self-worth, and to hate ignorance, backwardness, stupidity, and all forms of complacency. Our students were never to allow themselves to become satisfied until
they had achieved the highest possible goals and honors that
their mental and physical capabilities would allow.

Unfortunately, district school desegregation shadowed our
Beck High School plans. For example, in January 1970, I conducted two faculty meetings in one day. The morning meeting
was to say good-bye to my high school staff. The afternoon
meeting was to say hello and welcome to my 98% white junior
high school staff. Moments before going into the afternoon's
meeting, spooky thoughts of my "nigger mentality" surfaced.
"Oh my God! Those white women are going to kill me or they
will have me killed."

I mustered sufficient courage to enter the meeting room,
greeted the staff, and introduced short and long range goals
for our Beck Junior High School. The curriculum was simply
the same seventh grade program that we had always conducted
at Beck School. They smiled and some of them said, "Mr.
Stevenson, we fully understand the situation here, and we are
amply prepared to cope with this school organizational transi-
tion." To my delightful surprise, they were the smartest and
most professional human beings, who just happened to be
white, that I have ever met. Their dedicated, compelling, and
solid support shall never be forgotten.

Although I am fully aware that I have helped many white
and black people in Greenville, I have been triply blessed beyond human imagination because of my efforts to be helpful to
others. In 1971, we planned and implemented the new non-

graded team planning, and team teaching middle school concept, which included some open spaced classrooms for large
group instruction. Our staff and student body doubled, and
we were able to hire several nongraded teacher specialists from
the University of Pittsburgh. I also recruited teachers from the
Upper St. Clare School District, which had been labeled as having the most outstanding nongraded middle school in the country.

I spent two days in the Pittsburgh area studying their school
program. At this point, Beck was the largest middle school in
the district. Several of my staunch critics from the central administration declared the Beck Middle School faculty to be the
most outstanding, in every way, they had ever experienced. I
was surprised at their comments, because they had said and
done everything in their power to help insure failure of the
Beck Middle School project.

One of the major problems was people being bitterly opposed to innovative change. The dictionary, in its efforts to
clarify the meaning of innovation, was right when it said, "many
people are opposed to innovation, and it is difficult to innovate
when people feel that the old familiar way of doing something
is better." Previous to my promotion to the new Middle School
concept, I had been commended by at least two top central
office administrators as being the strongest principal in the
Greenville School District.

Beck's initial middle school plan was based on exemplary
middle schools in Mt. Kiska, New York, and Upper St. Clare
School District located in the Pittsburgh, Pennsylvania, area. The
entire project was under the jurisdiction and direction of the
Director of Elementary Education. He arranged for intensive training and nationwide travel for a select group of middle school
principals. He appeared to be fully committed to a full scale
nongraded middle school program. I was elated to have been

included in his study, traveling and action research group.

Visiting exemplary middle schools, nationwide, was the most exciting experience for me since my University of Missouri training. Unfortunately, intensive criticism from many sources derailed Greenville central administration of essential unwavering support necessary to help ensure success of the exemplary middle school project. Others were being blamed for problems connected with the project, including my superintendent. He had nothing to do with it.

My administrative staff and I put the Beck program together, and I assumed full responsibility for it. My emphatic resolve to implement the most flexible, efficient, and effective middle school program for our Beck students was not reversible. However, controversy erupted over nongraded versus the traditional graded lock-step program. Some members of our superior, dynamic faculty were split over the situation, and several parents felt that we simply were not ready for this drastic curriculum organizational change.

After serving one year with the Greenville Middle School project, the Pottstown School District, located in Pottstown, Pennsylvania, heard of my impelling motivation to establish and implement a nongraded school, recruited me for their school system. Unable to think of another innovative project to promote in Greenville that would be equal to or superior to the proposed Beck Middle School nongraded project, I accepted the Pottstown School District's offer and moved my family to Pottstown.

)()()()()()(

There was absolutely nothing inferior about the Beck High School program, facilities, students, and philosophy, compared to white high schools in the Greenville, South Carolina School

District. Therefore, closing Beck High School in the name of desegregation, was a mistake, unfair, unacceptable, and a travesty of justice to the black and white Nicholtown communities. The national NAACP in general and the local NAACP in particular must assume major responsibility for that inexcusable blunder.

According to H.G. Wells, in his book *The Outline of History*, 1956, most of Adolf Hitler's statements about his superiority, the superiority of the Nazi's, statements about his education, ambitions, and military achievements are either absolute lies or bold distortions of facts. As a school boy, Hitler was a complete failure, and he was unable to qualify to enter the art school of the Vienna Academy. He is considered the biggest liar the world has ever known. However, the NAACP's contention that all black public schools, regardless of extenuating circumstances, were inferior to all white schools was a prevarication far superior to anything Adolf Hitler ever dreamed of promoting.

Locally, it was also an inexcusable destruction of responsibility, self-esteem, self-help, school pride, and solid school support demonstrated by the Nicholtown black community. Even though this particular black community was poor, for some unexplainable reason they did not perceive themselves as being poor, and I simply could not find a concentration of the nigger mentality at the Beck High School.

Beck students were not afraid of anything or anybody. They were intelligent, academically gifted, and highly successful in accomplishing anything they set their minds to. The 120 piece marching band—indisputably the best we ever heard of anywhere in the world, and the undefeated state championship basketball team are two concrete examples. I am also told that Beck High School graduates are top engineers, ministers, teachers, business executives, journalists, professional speech writers, and entertainers such as Peabo Bryson.

Ernest "Bonecrusher" Hamilton was academically brilliant, a fierce football linesman at Beck High School, and further educated at the University of South Carolina and Michigan State University. He was constantly "Who's Who Among College Students" throughout the nation and is now Assistant District Attorney in the city of Greenville. If anything, Beck High School was superior to white high schools in the district because Beck met the same competitive, innovative, and exemplary standards of other schools with less than half as much financial support.

All funding for materials and minor supplementary equipment came from student fees. Less than half of Beck's students were financially able to pay the student fees. We were, therefore, compelled to do much more with less. We also found ourselves involved in colossal fund raising projects.

The Beck school situation is a supreme example of the contention that quality education is not necessarily based upon the amount of available funds or the size of the total budget. Beck School provided solid support for my contention that if the public school building principal would dare lead, the professional and nonprofessional staff, students, parents, and community, regardless of race, would follow. Being an effective principal is not easy, but, with courage and sustained perseverance, it can definitely be accomplished. Also, if teachers will teach, all students, regardless of race, will learn.

The NAACP is to be honored and praised for its efforts to ensure the continuation of the Lincoln University, located in Jefferson City, Missouri. Due to desegregation, Lincoln University was scheduled to be closed, and its students would be given the opportunity to attend the University of Missouri, which is located in Columbia, Missouri. Fortunately, the Lincoln school was labeled, "The school too good to close." Thanks to the NAACP and others, it is integrated, and remains one of the most honored and prestigious universities in the country.

The exact same thing should have happened to the Beck High School.

All changes, even those that appear to be drastically unfair, evil, and unjust, can be turned into a profound God-sent blessing for all concerned. For example, the current Beck school, fully integrated with at least 1,000 6th through 8th grade students, 59 member administrative and teaching staff, well maintained and improved building facilities, can perhaps do an even better job of indoctrinating the students with the will to excel in English, math, science, social studies, computer assist instruction, radio, closed circuit television, speech, dramatics, music, band, industrial arts, art, and all intramural sports.

Also, the principles of honor, respect for hard work, self-discipline, responsibility, love and respect for self, pride, and honor in exemplary achievement, self-dignity, respect for the rights of others, and the distinct advantages of pursuing love over hate are just as important for white students as they are for black students. Further, middle school students could be a bit more conducive to the rigid pressures and sustained perseverance required for maximum achievement in all outlined areas.

A biracial club could and should be organized, through which a tax deductible fund is established, in which the interest from the fund would be used to recognize the two students, regardless of race, who demonstrate the highest degree of mastery of agreed upon academic and nonacademic principles.

Chapter Eight

Pottstown: Third Mountaintop

L ife is constantly saying to each and everyone of us that "all things are possible, only believe." Life is and always has been big. It has no respect or sympathy for small insignificant things. It teaches us to aim high. Go for the sun. In the event it becomes necessary to settle for the moon or maybe a star, we still will have accomplished the impossible.

)()()()()(

In early May 1972, a delegation of educators from the Pottstown School District visited the Beck School for the purpose of interviewing me, talking with my superiors, talking with teachers in the schools, interviewing students, making a complete tour of the school, visiting my home, and making a general tour of the Greenville area. These school officials had heard, through a minister from Harrisburg, Pennsylvania, of my motivation to organize and conduct a nongraded school project.

Pottstown was already committed to the nongraded concept and simply wanted to find out if I might be a suitable candidate for their school system. They were also concerned about my possible interest in conducting a nongraded school in Pottstown. In reality, it was a thorough, intensive, and invigorating interview. However, it was conducted in the most relaxed, informal, and professional manner. We all felt highly honored and flattered to have Pennsylvania educators visit our school for whatever reason.

I cannot honestly say that, during the interviewing process, I was highly excited about the possibility of going to Pottstown, Pennsylvania. I had never heard of Pottstown, had no idea of where it was located, and I was concentrating on the possibility of securing employment in San Francisco, California. I had already made some contacts in San Francisco when I conducted a workshop on faculty meetings during the National Association of High School Principals several years earlier. My performance was considered highly successful and effective and I was quoted in the National Principals Magazine. Several California school officials talked with me about the possibility of working in the California area.

During the end of May 1972, my family and I were given the opportunity to visit Pottstown. We were shocked and highly surprised that it was not a huge inner city community like Baltimore, Philadelphia, and New York. We found that Pottstown had all of the advantages, benefits, and excitements of the major inner cities of the northeast without the inner city problems. The 40 mile ride west of Philadelphia from the airport was surrounded by the most beautiful and scenic landscapes of our experience. We were even more excited about the beauty of the immediate Pottstown area.

On June 3, 1972, my picture appeared in the Pottstown local newspaper along with an article stating:

> A middle school principal from Greenville, South Carolina, with ten years experience in school administration, will be

hired Monday as Principal of Jefferson School and will become the first black administrator in the Pottstown School District. Lemmon Stevenson, who was principal of elementary, junior, and senior high schools before taking the middle school post, also taught elementary school six years before going into administrative work. He will begin at Jefferson in early July. A 1952 graduate of South Carolina State College, he received a Masters of Science Degree in Education with a minor in Elementary Education six years later.

Since then, he earned 32 credits in Educational Administration from the University of Missouri where he studied during the summers of 1958 through 1961 and the school year 1961-62. An army veteran, Stevenson taught at Mitford Elementary School in South Carolina six years before becoming Principal of Elizabeth Heights School. After three years there, he became Principal of Beck Junior-Senior High School in Greenville for five years, followed by one year at Beck Junior High and the last year at Beck Middle School. For the past two years he was on the Greenville Government Study Commission to prepare recommendations for modernizing local government.

He was a leader in the Chamber of Commerce Government Modernization Committee which proposed the formation of the commission and served on executive boards of the United Fund and the YMCA.

He was Vice-Chairman of the Urban Work Committee, a church affiliated interdenominational organization.

Stevenson, the father of five children, will move to this area during the summer. His wife is teaching at Augusta Circle Elementary School.

My wife, Cecile, obtained employment as a fourth grade teacher in the Boyertown School District, which is 12 miles north of Pottstown. She was the first and only black teacher who has ever worked in the Colebrookdale Elementary School. However, she has never thought of herself as a black or white teacher, and the surrounding atmosphere of "whiteism" simply did not phase her. She always thought of herself as a good, solid, professional teacher. She had already done a superb job as first grade teacher for three years in the 90% white Augusta Circle Elementary School in the city of Greenville.

The parents of Ceclie's Greenville students were very upset when they found out that she would be leaving. She was very well received in her new school environment and apparently she continued to do an excellent job. Her principals appreciated her services, her colleagues loved her, and she received solid support from the parents of her children.

Pottstown

Pottstown, Pennsylvania, which is located in Montgomery County and 40 miles west of Philadelphia, Pennsylvania, is, without question, one of the most historic, cultural, economic, socially integrated, scenic, and educationally minded areas in this nation, and perhaps the world. It is three hours from New York City, three hours from Washington, D.C., two hours from Atlantic City, N.J., 15 minutes from Valley Forge and King of Prussia, and 15 minutes from Reading, Pennsylvania, a legendary industrial railroad and shopping center.

Pottstown is a humanitarian community and deliverer of its people, especially during a crisis, which was evident in the devastating flood of 1972. The loss of major industry in the area, such as Firestone, Bethlehem Steel, and others, are concrete examples. Pottstown loves, respects, supports, defends, and honors its own. Accordingly, Pottstown has always (and I believe it always will) bounced back stronger than ever before from any crisis or unforeseen hardship. It emphasizes unity, brotherhood, peace, justice, cooperation, and good-will over hate, evil, and violence.

Pottstown has a good school system. I have been highly impressed with the effectiveness of Pottstown Senior High School. Although it has received some unfair and unrealistic criticisms, it has been extremely effective and efficient in preparing young people, regardless of race, creed, or economic conditions, for whatever future endeavors of their choice. My three daughters are graduates of this honorable high school. Anita, our oldest daughter, is a pharmacist in Columbia, South Carolina. Because of her superior high school training, her first year in college was simply a review of what she learned in high school.

Our second oldest daughter, Donna, is an engineer in Rochester, New York. Her first year college experience was very similar to that of Anita's. Loretta, our youngest daughter, selected one of the most challenging universities in Pennsylvania. She did very well, but personal matters interrupted her college education prior to graduation. The Pottstown High School has done its job extremely well for my children and for thousands of others who are providing honorable and essential services to mankind all over this nation.

Pottstown is basically a godly community consisting of many churches, synagogues, and other established Christian experiences. One of my first and foremost enduring experiences in Pottstown was a visit to the new stone constructed Second Baptist Church. The 600 capacity church with a basement capacity of 300 persons was approximately 95% complete during my 1972 visit. The singing and preaching were among the best I had ever heard. Many of the performers, during this period of time, have passed on. However, they have left an unforgettable legacy. Mr. Glenices Taylor was a concrete example of the best spiritual singer of that time. Mr. Harold Johnson is another of the old type great spiritual singers. He is alive and still performing at his peak level. Reverend David Minus, who is now retired, is one of the greatest, traditional spiritual singers and preachers.

The most astounding reality of this new stone Second Baptist Church is that it was and still is debt free. There was never a mortgage. All construction debts were paid as they occurred. The business executive and financial genius who planned, organized, and initiated this highly unusual and successful project was the honorable Haywood Butler, the most dynamic pastor in the history of the Second Baptist Church. When the church was completely framed, boxed in with a complete top, the original contractor went bankrupt.

More determined than ever before to complete the church project, Reverend Butler secured the services of building contractor Mr. R. B. Hunter, who persuaded Reverend Butler to serve as chaplain of the semi-pro football team known as the Firebirds. Reverend Butler was so effective in stimulating and motivating the Firebirds semi-pro football team that the team pledged to do whatever it could to help insure the financial success of Reverend Butler's Second Baptist Church. The following letter from the United States White House confirms the solid unity and cooperation existing among contractor, Mike Hunter, Reverend Butler, and the Firebirds football team.

THE WHITE HOUSE
Washington, D.C.

August 25, 1969
Dear Mr. Hunter:

I am writing on behalf of the President to commend the members of the Brotherhood Bowl Committee and all the other people who so generously are contributing their time and effort to assist the Second Baptist Church complete the construction of its new church complex.

The President feels strongly that only when people are able to share with and assist one another spontaneously and without thought of reward can there be true brotherhood and harmony. The work of the people of Pottstown on behalf of the Second Baptist Church has brought us one step closer to that goal. Let us hope that other communities will learn from this important example.

Sincerely yours,

Bruce Rabb
Staff Assistant to The President

It has been said that we should give to the world the best that we have and the best will come back to us. Mike Hunter's humanitarian version of this old saying is, "Give to the world all that you have and hope and pray for self and family survival." I have never met a humanitarian like Mike Hunter. He agreed to complete the Second Baptist Church at a cost of 10% of what would normally be charged for such a huge project. When the work was completed, Mike presented the church with a bill for the 10% along with a check which covered the exact amount of the bill. He also gave the church several additional thousands of dollars to help ensure its success, wherever that money may have been needed.

Mike's generosity to the Second Baptist Church brought hostile and vicious verbal attacks from some Second Baptist Church members and also many other Pottstown citizens and Mike's associates who simply could not understand why he would do so much for a community that did not or perhaps could not fully understand and appreciate what he was doing.

Mike Hunter passed away May 14, 1996. During his funeral services, the current chairman of the Second Baptist Church education committee read a resolution honoring Mike for his solid and unwavering financial support of the church. I was extremely proud, happy and excited over the reality that Mike Hunter had finally received public recognition for his humanitarian services to the church. My excitement in this matter is based upon the sad, indefensible, bias, and racist verbal attack level against Mike by the then chairman of the church's educational committee when Mike offered to establish a $50,000 scholarship fund for the youth of the Second Baptist Church. This chairperson yelled, "We don't want any white person raising money for our church."

The church officials supported the chairman. Mike had agreed to put up $50,000 of his own money and with the help and support of several of his rich white friends and associates, he would raise an additional $75,000. As a member of this education committee, I was startled. I knew and thought the church leaders knew that the only future the Second Baptist Church had was the young people. Also, without education, the Pottstown community and state are doomed. Also, for adverse racism to be allowed to raise its ugly head and succeed, in a church that actually owes it existence to biracial support, was more than I could endure.

I resigned from the education committee, and I sincerely hope and pray that I will never support or endeavor to defend a racist cause. We are all God's children, regardless of race, nationality, or gender, and we must learn how to live and work together, whether we like it or not. It is our only salvation.

Perhaps the most respected, honorable, and effective longevity minister in the Pottstown area is the Reverend Martin L. Acker of Emmanuel Lutheran Church located in the city of Pottstown. I learned to love, appreciate, and truly respect the services provided to me and the Pottstown community by Reverend Acker and his congregation.

Chapter Nine

The Eagle—A Powerful and Inspiring Motivator

I t is an indisputable fact that the bald eagle is the most powerfully skilled flyer in the world. Also, because of the eagle's strength, love for and demonstrated determination to be free, the founders of the United States of America selected it for the national emblem.

)()()()(

As Director of School Desegregation for the Pottstown School District, it became my duty and responsibility to merge black and white students in three of the district's five elementary schools. This voluntary integration process included children in grades kindergarten through six. At the same time, I was also to serve as principal of Rupert Elementary School; one of the three newly integrated schools.

Rupert's mission was clear, precise, and indisputably compelling. Staff professionalism, student behavior, and overall academic achievement were expected to surpass the school's already outstanding performance records. Most importantly, Rupert was also to serve as a role model for the Pottstown School District, the State of Pennsylvania, and the Nation.

Accordingly, my first official act as principal of Rupert Elementary School was to send out a three question survey to parents, teachers, and non-instructional staff. They were asked to answer all questions and return the survey to me by a specified date. They were informed that it was not necessary for them to sign the survey form. I wanted their input to help me devise a suitable educational program for our students. The questions I presented were: (1) What do you like best about your school? (2) What do you like least about your school? (3) What do you think we should do collectively to correct any existing school problems?

Surprisingly, 100 percent of the Rupert parents returned the survey, and they all signed it, including addresses and telephone numbers. Although most teachers and staff did not sign the survey, the returns from them were also 100%, and I received sufficient input to go forward with the program.

Although the Rupert School parent were primarily concerned about the academic achievement of their students, there has always been a prevailing belief that integration of black students causes a deterioration (or even total breakdown) of academic achievement, student responsibility, and discipline. Accordingly, my staff and I were confronted with the challenging task of making sure every Rupert student knew and understood that he/she was expected to achieve academically to the maximum level of his/her abilities. Therefore, it was imperative that we develop and implement an outstanding student self-esteem and self-motivation project.

Learning is an individual process and each student must do his own learning. I began by involving the students in choosing a new school mascot to replace the existing mascot, a rooster. During a planning meeting with first, second, and fourth grade students, one of our first grade girls asked, "Mr. Stevenson, is a rooster a chicken?" My answer was, "Yes." The student then responded, "There is no way in the world we will ever be chicken. That rooster will have to go!"

This opened the floor for new mascot nominations. Because the classic movie "Charlotte's Web" was very popular in our district, one of our fourth graders suggested that we select a spider. Several second graders yelled, "No way!" Other suggestions followed, including the Trojan (Pottstown High School's mascot), bear, lion, tiger, cougar, panther, whale, falcon, and eagle. I decided to provide committee of students with three days to read and study these animals and to reduce the nominees to three. The total student body would then vote on three selections.

It was apparent that the eagle was an early favorite, as several students volunteered to write and deliver speeches about what it meant to be an eagle. Some of their comments were: "An eagle is smart, an eagle is wise, and all eagles are daring and courageous; an eagle is not afraid of anything; an eagle is kind and peaceful, but if you mess with an eagle, you will be crushed and clawed to bits; all eagles have to learn how to be the best flyers in the world; young eagles that are too scared or too lazy to learn how to fly will be kicked out of the nest by their parents; eagles are the best fishermen in the world, and no small animal like a rat, rabbit, or snake can hide or run away from an eagle's attack."

With the first and second graders as the largest voting blocs, a landslide vote for the eagle resulted. The content of our student speeches, and the manner in which they were delivered, convinced me beyond a reasonable doubt that an eagle's motivational power was extremely effective. Students were making comments such as, "I can do anything or be anything I want to be; I am just as good and just as important as anybody else in the whole world; all I have to do is make up my mind what it is that I want to do and then work at it as hard as I possibly can; my school grades can definitely be B's and A's instead of C's and D's."

The golden eagle was the emblem of the Roman legions. "The largest eagles are the Herpy Eagle of South America, and the Philippine Eagle, whose wingspans reach eight feet (2.4 m).

Symbolically, as the student body became Eagles, their attitudes and behavior changed dramatically. One outstanding example of this attitude change was that our students began to assume responsibility for their conduct in school, and on their way to and from school. We were able to conduct student body assemblies without the presence and supervision of classroom teachers. At this point, the assemblies were planned, implemented, and evaluated by the students themselves.

Our most amazing and unforgettable assemblies occurred once per year to celebrate pride in ourselves, our home, our school, and our community. The annual event was called Dress-Up Day, and every one of our students would dress in their "Sunday go to meeting" clothing. The assembly was conducted during recess so that the students would not have the opportunity to go out on the playground and possibly damage or dirty their best clothing. The students had to assume full responsibility for their conduct because the teachers were having lunch in another part of the building. The principal and two playground aides were the only adults in attendance.

Parents were invited, and some did attend. Sometimes, the guidance counselor and music teachers would volunteer their time and services. All of our special student assemblies were videotaped by our guidance counselor, Mr. Fine.

As Eagles, the Rupert School family directed a vicious attack against mediocrity, irresponsibility, excuse making, blaming others for our problems, and allowing ourselves to be crippled and defeated by the word "can't." We declared war on backwardness and fear of academic competition. Our students realized that they were just as good as anybody in the world and could compete favorably in district speech and math competitions, and even in state and national standardized test competitions.

I am reminded of one district-wide math competition in which Rupert's five member fourth grade team scored 88 points higher than the second place team in the district. Our five member fifth grade team scored 80 points higher than the second place team. That year, Rupert School's math teams were honored at a special School Board meeting for being the best math teams in the district. Rupert earned the reputation of being the best school in mathematics in the district.

Another feather in the Eagles' cap was the establishment and promotion of the first district-wide computer lab. Then we established and promoted our own radio and closed circuit television project.

Today, many of our Eagles are students in, or have already graduated from, some of the greatest colleges and universities in America. Former Rupert Eagles are now lawyers, doctors, engineers, and school teachers. The unique, aggressive, and profound performance of the Rupert School students, parents, community, and professional staff, is a triumph of the American Dream at its best.

At the national level, the eagle represents life, beauty, strength, courage, loyalty, responsibility, and freedom for every human being in every state of this nation. Accordingly, we sent this vital message out to all the world: Rupert School, which is located on South and Mount Vernon Streets in Pottstown, Pennsylvania, is too good to be closed! Why would anybody in his right mind want to close the best school in the district?

There is another part of this message, and it comes directly from the hearts of Rupert School Eagles. If there is any family, anywhere in the world, whose children would like to attend the best school in America, simply move your entire family to Pottstown, Pennsylvania, and establish residence in the Rupert Elementary School attendance area. A countless number of families have done this, and they have never regretted it.

THE RUPERT SCHOOL EAGLE FUND
by
Lemmon Stevenson, Retired Principal
Myra Forrest, Principal
James R. Bush, Business Administrator
February 28, 1997

The Eagle Fund, established in 1997 by the former and current principals, and supported by faculty, former students, and parents of the Rupert School, is a unique and powerful student motivator. The award is based upon innovative projects which produced outstanding student achievements between 1981 and 1991. Many of these students are teachers, lawyers, doctors, and top business executives. The award is designed to help current and future young students know and understand that they can be real winners at being and doing anything they set their minds to. Students must set high goals and demonstrate sufficient effort to reach them. They must be positive and never give up. "Winners never quit and quitters never win!"

The awards will consist of a United States Savings Bond designed to help finance the students' future education. The amounts of the U.S. Savings Bonds will be determined by the interest earned on the principal of the award fund for the year the award is given. The bonds will be issued to the two students, at the exit grade, who demonstrate a high degree of mastery and utilization of the following guidelines and good citizenship principles:

1. Must spend at least two full years at the Rupert Elementary School before graduation. (Currently fourth and fifth grades.)

2. Must demonstrate a positive and constructive attitude about school work and also his/her relationships with teachers and other students.

3. Must demonstrate responsibility for his/her behavior during the school day and also on the way to and from school. (Self-Discipline)

4. Must demonstrate necessary courage and perseverance to work on extremely challenging tasks, and if failure occurs, be willing to start again and work harder to achieve success. (Never give up.)

5. Must be academically competitive with other students at the local, state, and national levels, as measured by standardized tests. Student's overall school grades must be good to superior.

The student selection will be done by the appropriate classroom teachers, the guidance counselor, and the building principal.

The fund, which is open for tax deductible contributions from teachers, administrators, former students, parents, community, and anyone else willing to contribute, is expected to exceed $30,000.00. The initial fund is $5,100.00. Contributions to the fund at this time are sincerely appreciated. The fund will be invested and only the interest will be awarded to qualifying students.

Checks should be made payable to the Pottstown School District - "Rupert Eagle Award."

Chapter Ten

Equality of Performance Requirements

T he will and determination to survive and succeed in our chosen profession must be stronger than any obstacles or hardships anyone can level against us. Life is not fair and it has always been a struggle. However, there is always a bright side to life. The challenges and disappointments in our lives should be used to prepare us for the next higher level of challengers. Life is a continuous process from the cradle to the grave and every level of progress on life's journey, is much more difficult and challenging than ever before.

)()()()()()(

When I became Principal of Jefferson School, I had already experienced and successfully overcome hundreds of major setbacks, insurmountable obstacles, major disappointments, and risks. Accordingly, the challenges and obstacles I anticipated in Pottstown, Pennsylvania, compared to the Greenville, South Carolina, challenges were like going on a fun and games picnic.

What I did not know and understand was the different educational, political, social, and economic differences existing between Greenville, South Carolina, and Pottstown, Pennsylvania. For example, I had never heard of unions in the school system. In Greenville, the principals, superintendent, and teachers belonged to and participated in the same teacher organization. Another difference was that my colleagues in Pottstown held masters and doctorate degrees and were graduates from some of the largest and most prestigious colleges in the Northeast and perhaps in this nation. They had all been exposed to the greatest elementary, secondary, and college educational opportunities and privileges America had to offer.

How in the world should I ever, realistically, be expected to compete favorably with them? My boss and district superintendent, Dr. Ray E. Feick, had the answer to my question. I suggested to him that I may have some difficulty competing favorably with my northern colleagues. He told me, "Lemmon, you are expected and you will compete, not only with all of your colleagues, but you are going to compete with me. We know what you can do, we want you in our school system, and you are expected to perform in accordance with our expectations."

Defensibly, he simply could not have said anything else. I am eternally grateful to him for allowing me an equal chance to perform in his school system. Accordingly, I simply cannot think of any serious or major problem of competition involving other district administrators and myself. All of my major Pottstown School District goals and objectives, except one, were far above and beyond minimum requirements of my district administrative contractual agreement.

Some of my goals included major building renovation, desegregation of elementary schools, minority teacher recruitment, director of state and federal programs, school computer labs, school close-circuit television, and non-graded team teaching. Although I was contracted to conduct one non-graded primary school, the other six projects were extra and above the normal call of duty. My major problems, criticism, and objections came as a result of my endeavoring to do too much too soon. I was constantly reprimanded for pushing too hard to accomplish too much. "Lemmon, you are moving too fast. The world was not made in one day. You have just arrived in Pottstown."

Some of my staff members were very unhappy and offended by my philosophy and demonstrated commitment to do three or more extra jobs without requiring or demanding extra pay for extra work. One of the minority teachers thought that my willingness to operate the largest elementary school in the district and also direct state and federal programs, which included another staff equal in size of the elementary school, was absurd. Other associates of mine have used adjectives that were much sharper, specific and very easy to understand, such as unintelligent, dumb, Uncle Tomish, backward, naive, and stupid.

My philosophy of being willing to work twice as hard, if necessary, as my competitors to meet the educational needs of my students leaked out among my staff. Some community leaders approached me about the matter. Although I have always defended my actions to the best of my abilities, I have never explained my working philosophy to anybody prior to this written report.

Perhaps the best way for me to explain and defend my work conviction is to raise and answer the following question. Why have I been so willing and anxious to do extra work projects designed to help meet the educational needs of our young people? In the first place, I have been a young American citizen who experienced considerable difficulty at every level of my schooling. Accordingly, I feel an overpowering obligation and commitment to do everything I possibly can to help other young American school children experience love, acceptance,

Albert Richburg, Assistant Principal, Beck High School, 1967.

"an invaluable professional administrator"

Joseph E. Beck High School, 1967.
"Second Mountaintop"

Beck High School Dedication Meeting, 1965.

*Parent-Teachers Association Meeting at Elizabeth Heights School,
Great Falls, S.C., 1965.*

*Mitford School
Faculty*

*Mitford Elementary
and Junior High
School*

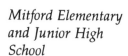

Jefferson Elementary School Staff

Reverend Hayward Butler (L) and Mike Hunter (R)
"Inseparable"

Second Baptist Church (partially completed structure)

*Second Baptist Church (finished structure
under direction of Mike Hunter).*

*W. W. Rupert School
"Third Mountaintop"*

*W. W. Rupert Elementary
School Staff*

*"Young Eagles at Rupert School—
the ultimate challenge."*

Franklin School Elementary Staff, 1978-1979

Franklin School, 1979

support, responsible discipline, academic success, and the joy of our public school system.

Secondly, and most importantly, I learned as a college student that work is the most important single value this world has to offer. I also learned from my successful school projects in South Carolina, how to truly love and appreciate the glory, excitement, respectability, and satisfactions resulting from recruiting more than 200 school teachers for three school districts in South Carolina and participation in the renovation of one traditional and the construction of two new modern innovative schools.

This satisfaction also included teaching and directing a nongraded elementary school for six years, conducting innovative school lunch programs in which every child was guaranteed a lunch each day for five years, conducting a pre and post standardized psychological testing program for five years, and placing many economically deprived students in various colleges and universities on full college scholarships.

I am quite sure there must have been many individuals who could have done a better job with Title I, school desegregation, and staff recruitment, in the Pottstown School District, than I did. However, I simply did not see a single one of those individuals when I voluntarily took over those extra assignments. Therefore, it became not only an opportunity, but an obligation for me to take on those challenging humanitarian causes. I did not request, did not want, and did not consider extra money. I had already been given a good initial salary, which included substantial raises each year.

Also, I had been doing eight times more innovative work in South Carolina with less money than I had been requested to do in Pottstown. I was also highly honored to have been considered for a job in Pottstown. In fact, I would have gladly done the assignments at no pay, if I had been financially able to afford it. There are some things in this world that are more important than money. Happiness and enjoyment of exciting work are concrete examples.

Not only did Pottstown allow me to continue my exciting, innovative work, which included extensive state and national travel, but it also afforded me the most outstanding professional staff of workers to be found anywhere in the world. Outstanding staff members included school librarians, school registered nurses, guidance counselors, school psychologists, and more than 14 reading and math specialists.

I am convinced, beyond a reasonable doubt, that the school administrator or teacher who is saturated with the notion that he or she should get rich by draining school districts of every possible nickel, should consider some other line of work. The question should never be, "What can and will my school district do for me, but rather what can and will I do for my school district." Our school systems are in critical need for humanitarian services from its employees—not greed. Sincere school district personnel must set realistic goals and do everything they possibly can to help ensure a better life for our current and future young people.

The final words on this section include comments by the honorable Dr. Benjamin E. Mays, who was former president of Moorehouse College located in Atlanta, Georgia. He contended that a good, meaningful life is to be judged by accomplished deeds or results rather than rhetoric. It is summarized in what Dr. Mays called *God's Minute.*

I have only just a minute, only 60 seconds in it, forced upon me; couldn't refuse it, didn't seek it, didn't choose it, but it is up to me to use it. I must suffer if I lose it, give account if I abuse it. Just a tiny little minute, but eternity is in it.

The above poem, which Dr. Mays found in an unidentified newspaper, should be a reflection of all of us. It means that we must allow no sand to burn under our feet and that no one has ever built a reputation on what he or she is **going** to do. It is what we **do** that counts and we should be ashamed to die before making a worthwhile contribution to mankind. Also, we must be aware of the possibility that life's end may be much closer than we realize.

Chapter Eleven

Can Anything Good Come Out of the South?

*H*istory tells us that this world is and always has been saturated with love, hate, good and evil. Therefore, the question should not be, "Can anything good come out of the South? The question should be, "To what extent are we willing to identify, document, and communicate the indisputable good and honor from the South?" Thus, the purpose of this chapter is to address this latter question.

)()()()()(

The South, which is generally referred to as the territories below the Mason-Dixon line, has been discussed and evaluated by numerous groups, individuals, and people of different races. Some of the common remarks I hear about the people of the South are absurd, such as all southern whites, as well as blacks, are ignorant and stupid and southern white people are mean, evil, racist, and hate-mongers toward blacks.

On the other side of the same contention, people (mainly from "up North") say that all northern white people are kind, lovable, do-gooders, non-racists, wise, very intelligent, educated, and they are extremely receptive and helpful to Negroes. Northern black people are smart, free of oppressions, well-educated, have good jobs, fine homes, nice automobiles, and lots of money to spend, while living the good life.

Many years ago, I recall hearing the statement, "I would rather know less than to know so much that ain't so." This quote supposedly came from the so-called, "simple philosopher." I was born and reared in the South. I knew, firsthand, what the South was like during the 30's, 40's, 50's, and 60's. I also know what the South is like in the 90's. I have also lived and worked in the North. Accordingly, the above pack of transparent lies, deceptions, and misrepresentations make a review of them, pertaining to my personal experiences, imperative.

During the early 60's, I recall hearing a TV program in which it was announced that four of the greatest news commentators in America were not only from the South, but they were from South Carolina, my home state. One of them was Frank Blair. Another one was David Brinkley, who is still working in the news business. I do not recall the names of the other two. However, I can never forget the excitement, pride, and honor I felt for those men and also my native state. The fact that they were white made absolutely no difference to me. I was truly overjoyed. Frank Blair was truly and indisputably awesome in his ability to organize and deliver the news of this world.

During the late 50's, a university professor from Harvard University conducted a seminar at the University of Missouri. I was there. This professor said, among other things, there are 600 known superior black educators in this country. Also, all 600 came from below the Mason-Dixon line except three. Alabama produced the largest number of the 600 educators. Mississippi was second, and the state of Georgia was third. Others were distributed throughout the South. This professor did not name the individual educators, but Dr. Benjamin E. Mays, native of South Carolina, winner of a Phi Beta Kappa Key, awarded the

Ph.D. Degree from the University of Chicago, and President of Moorehouse College in Atlanta, Georgia, would have had to be one of the 600. Dr. Mays was also author of at least 20 books.

Another one of the 600 would have no doubt been Dr. Mordecai Johnson, 1890-1976. Dr. Johnson, native of Tennessee, earned a Masters Degree from Harvard University in 1923 and the Doctor of Divinity Degree from Gammon Theological Seminary in 1928. He was president of Howard University, in Washington, D.C., for more than 30 years, beginning in 1926. Howard University, under his leadership, became the first and only true Negro university in America.

Dr. Johnson won the Spingarn Medal in 1929 for perpetuating Negro progress in America. Dr. Johnson was a staunch advocate and promoter of self-sufficiency, pride, and dignity of hard work and responsibility. During the late 40's, I heard him deliver a speech at South Carolina State College in which he stated, "Any person, regardless of race, who does not or will not work, should not eat."

The Harvard professor, during this University of Missouri seminar, delivered a devastating blow to the documented report that Booker T. Washington in education, George Washington Carver in science, Marion Anderson in music, and Joe Louis in sports, were the only Negroes who had accomplished anything worthy of being recorded in the history books of America. I was fascinated by this report because it confirmed one of my contentions that obstacles, along with an occasional kick in the pants, can be a profound self-motivator for any human being.

One of the most admirable and intensely dedicated professional business executives of my experience, who just happens to be from Lancaster, South Carolina, is Mr. Mike Duncan. Mike, a graduate of Morgan State University, entered the banking business and became Vice President and General Manager at a $25 billion corporation. He designed and implemented company-wide programs for management and nonmanagement employees.

Feeling that his talents were not being used effectively, Mike resigned from his prominent position and decided to form his own business, but not before first writing a very popular book titled, *Reach Your Goals in Spite of the Old Boy Network*. His research into the book publishing business uncovered voids that he did not like. Rather than negative moaning and groaning about the problems he encountered, he decided to form a book publishing firm, Duncan & Duncan, Inc., and introduce corrective competitive changes within the industry. His firm has published books by authors from around the country and primarily seeks material that helps people to accomplish their life's goal or mission. Mike took full advantage of available opportunities, but most admirably, he created new independent and unlimited opportunities for friends, associates, as well as for himself.

Never in the recorded history of this nation have we ever had an ignorant president. Jimmy Carter of Georgia was president of this nation and he is still doing a remarkable job pertaining to peace, justice, cooperation, and goodwill throughout the world. No president in the history of this nation has been a more effective humanitarian. Currently, William Clinton of Arkansas is President of the United States. He has always demonstrated the commitment and courage to do whatever is necessary to help ensure a healthy, economically viable, and militarily safe and secure nation. I perceive President Clinton as being fully committed and determined to bear any burden and pay any price to meet the needs he perceives to be essential for America.

U.S. Supreme Court Justice Clarence Thomas of Alabama and U.S. Office of Education Secretary Dick Reilly have been just as aggressive, efficient, and effective as others who have served in these capacities. Secretary Reilly is from South Carolina.

I would not think of ending this chapter without including at least two other indisputably humanitarian servants who just happen to be from the South. The first one is Mr. Fred Fowler who was Inter-City School Superintendent of Greenville, South Carolina. He was my boss and immediate supervisor for nine years. He served as high school principal of Greenville's oldest, largest and most prestigious high school before becoming superintendent. He was the essence of Mr. Professionalism and I have endeavored to be just like him. You always knew what was on his mind because he would tell you.

For example, when I became too pushy and overly aggressive in my determination to promote the best possible non-graded middle school, Mr. Fowler said to me and my two assistant principals, "You men are in trouble with this middle school program, but there is a positive side to your situation. You are all young and energetic enough to leave Greenville and go to one of those school districts that are searching for non-graded school principals. At my age, I am stuck with this situation." Oh did I forget to say that Mr. Fowler was also born and reared in the backwoods of Union County, South Carolina.

The other gentleman who must be listed is Dr. Thomas Kerns, the assertive and aggressive humanitarian who worked his way up from a student at the Old Sterling High School to earn a Ph.D. Degree and also became the first black superintendent of Greenville County School District. Dr. Kerns accomplished all of this in less than thirty years. Allow me to add that Dr. Kerns paid the full price for every ounce of his success. However, being required to pay the piper did not frighten or discourage Dr. Kerns. He simply kept traveling forward, non-stop until he reached his goals. Most respectfully, Dr. Kerns flatly refused to consider himself a black or white superintendent. In his own words, Dr. Kerns said, "I have never seen myself as a black superintendent. I'm a superintendent who happens to be black. Everything I do must be for the good of all children."

The most awesomely effective and respected Christian and

spiritual leader of modern times is the honorable Dr. Billy Graham. He has and is still preaching to millions of people worldwide through personal crusades, radio, television, newspapers, magazines, and several books written by him. Most importantly, he is owned, loved, and appreciated by the South. He was born and reared in Charlotte, North Carolina.

My first direct encounter with Dr. Graham occurred in the 50's when he flatly refused to conduct a segregated crusade in Columbia, South Carolina. The crusade was finally conducted on an integrated basis at the Fort Jackson Military Base. My family and I attended. It was the most exciting spiritual experience of our lives. At this point in time, all U.S. military bases, regardless of location, were integrated by executive order of United States' President Harry S. Truman. Thousands of excited and enthusiastic people attended that outdoor stadium crusade. Never before had I ever experienced a minister who quoted the Bible extemporaneously for hours. As an evangelist, Dr. Billy Graham is right up there with Matthew, Mark, Luke, and John—the writers of the Gospel found in the New Testament.

Although educational opportunities in the South for whites and blacks have not always been equal to or superior to those available to blacks and whites in the North, I am personally amazed at the national competitive performance of whites and blacks from the South. I have come to the conclusion that full utilization of available educational opportunities are, by far, more important than the availability of superior educational opportunities in which limited advantages are taken of these opportunities.

Chapter Twelve

Unforeseen Tragedy

I gnorance of the safe and secure laws of nature and man, combined with blind innocent trust and belief that everything will be all right positioned Henretta and me for the greatest shock of our lives—the total destruction of our farm home. Oh yes, we were fully aware of other families losing their homes to tornadoes, floods, earthquakes, bombings, and fire. However, those were things that happened to other people. We were too naive to think of such things happening to us, but because of our thoughtlessness, I am able to better understand and appreciate Rudyard Kipling's poem which says in part, "If you can bear to hear the truth you have spoken, twisted by knaves to make a trap for fools, or watch the things you gave your life to broken and stooped and built them up with worn out tools and so hold on when there is nothing in you except the will which says to them—hold on!"

)()()()()(

All of the problems, setbacks, disappointments, hardships, oppressions, and hostile vicious attacks leveled at the Stewart family and me, prior to January 12, 1986, were only dress rehearsals. I can think of nothing that would have fully prepared us for the tragic news that our old historic family home had been totally destroyed by fire. Everything the family had accumulated during the past 60 years was turned into ashes.

I was particularly concerned and upset about my high school through graduate school books, papers, special school projects, and other artifacts I had accumulated during my 18 months stay in Europe. Susan Stewart had constantly counseled us all that perhaps the banks and post offices could not, or at least should not, be trusted with all of the money in our possession. Accordingly, most of the family cash money was securely hidden in the house. This money was located in the most hideous places imaginable.

My mother, Ella, was a collector of antiques, many of which she collected during her stay in Harrisburg, PA. All of our beds were antiques. Several art collectors had offered the family several thousands of dollars for the antique beds, along with a guarantee of their replacements with new modern furniture. I begged my family to take advantage of the offer because they needed the money. However, the family refused to sell.

The fire, which completely destroyed the house, began around 9:00 A.M. and was finished around 10:15 P.M. The fire department came, along with police and a strong out-pour of neighbors and friends. They were able to save the chimney and two small houses which were located very close to the home.

Living in the house at the time of the fire were Ben, Henretta, and her nephew Gary Gladney. Henretta was in bed asleep, and Gary was in the guest room with a large fire going in the trash burner. It was extremely cold that night, and Gary, who had not gone to bed, was apparently sitting in a chair and had fallen asleep. When he woke up, the fire was already burning out of control between the chimney and wall of the room. Gary immediately threw water on the area, but to no avail. The fire was already out of control. He got Henretta out of bed, but she did not have time to put on any clothes. I received word of the fire the following day. Henretta was in hysterics. However, she was glad that Gary woke her up and did not allow her to be consumed by the fire.

My family and I lived in Pottstown, PA, and we offered Henretta the opportunity to move to Pennsylvania and live with us. She had previously lived with us when she took care of my children. However, Henretta insisted on continuing to live on the farm and, if possible, she wanted to live on the same home site. The only way that could be done, of course, was to build and furnish a new home. Here, we are talking about a major financial investment far superior to anything made by me back in 1947, when I put up $3,000 to purchase the farm.

The house had been a community meeting place for members of the family, and we had entertained our relatives and friends there during the deaths of Charlie, Susan, Robert, Ella, and also occasions during revival meetings at St. John's, Shady Grove, Red Hill, and Prospect Churches. My family and I were also concerned that we continued to have a place to stay when we visited Winnsboro. At that point in time, any visits we made to Winnsboro would require securing a hotel room or living with relatives.

Recognizing that we owned the property and had managed to avoid placing a mortgage against it, I decided to make another major investment in the property by building a house similar to the one that had been destroyed. Henretta stated that she would be happy if we could build her a one room concrete slab house. Commonly built houses in the county were concrete slab bungalows. I told Henretta I was not happy with the house that burned. Although major improvements had been made to upgrade the house, it was still an embarrassment to us, compared to the houses of many of our associates and friends.

However, I told her that if we could not build a house in which we all could be proud, we would not rebuild at all. My brother-in-law, Mansel Ross, and I reviewed several plans of interest. All of the plans I liked would cost more than $100,000 to construct. We finally selected a plan and used concrete blocks instead of blocks and brick. The insulation and interior finish would be the same as the more expensive homes, but the cost would be 5 to 10 percent cheaper. Mr. Ross is a builder who built a brick house for me and a fabulous brick house for himself during the 50's.

We decided to use the Winnsboro Building Supply and the H.Q. Company for all basic construction material. The four bedroom home was constructed within six to eight months. Meanwhile, Henretta was allowed to live in the home of a friend until her house was rebuilt. Her friend's home was approximately one mile from the destroyed farmhouse. Henretta visited the home site on a daily basis. She had several animals that required her care.

Chapter Thirteen

My Father—A Man of Courage and Dignity

T he certainty and uncompromising reality of death has visited the Stewart and Stevenson families on numerous occasions. My mothers (real and adopted), aunts, cousins, uncles, and brothers have all passed away. Death is the certainty that we will all confront at some point in time. My concerns pertaining to it have to do with the duty and responsibility of each and every one of us to love your enemies, do good to those who persecute you, feed the hungry, visit the sick, and defend truth, freedom, and the golden rule. Also, it is most important to know and understand that no one really benefits from acts of greed, hate, injustices, along with vicious and evil attacks on other humans.

I also like the words in the song that say: If I can help somebody as I travel along; if I can show somebody that he is traveling wrong; then my living will not have been in vain.

XXXXXX

I did not get to know or spend much time with my father. He was extremely busy earning a living and rearing his family. I, on the other hand, seemed always occupied learning how to survive in my newly adopted family, acquiring an education, and making a difference in the lives of my fellow man—especially young people. We were fully aware of each other's activities and occasionally conducted brief discussions on them.

I learned to love and respect my father as a saint. He was a man who always did the best he could with what he had. I never heard my father bellyache, gripe, or complain about how bad things were. He simply did what he had to do, the way he had to do it. He hoped for the best, worked for the best, but, in the end, he took what came. Most importantly, he took life's challenges with courage, grace, and dignity. This was especially true as he lay on his death bed dying from cancer.

He was extremely proud of me, not only because I was his son, but because I had finished college. He stated, on one occasion, "Lemmon, you have done all of this on your own. You had no money and your family was in no position to help you."

Although my father did not know or understand it, I have always had solid and unwavering support in all of my endeavors. Most of it came from unexpected and anonymous sources. Unfortunately, he did not live to see me become the principal of one of the largest, newest, and most modern high schools in the state of South Carolina. He and his sister Susan would have been overjoyed.

My father, several months before he died, made me executor of his estate. Part of my responsibilities included directing his funeral arrangements. He was a proud veteran of World War I. Accordingly, I secured the services of the army, which included a chaplain to deliver the eulogy. The message was clear, precise, consoling, liberating, and delivering. The echo of the chaplain's message still rings in my ears. "I will lift up mine eyes unto the hills . . . The Lord is my Shepherd; I shall not want . . . And I will dwell in the house of the Lord forever . . . Let not your hearts be troubled . . . In my Father's house are many mansions. I go to prepare a place for you—that where I am, there you may be also. So lived that when thy summons come . . . Approach thy grave like one who wraps the drapery of his couch about him, and lies down to pleasant dreams."

One church critic stated that the service was the most dignified ever held in that church. The usual fire and brimstone sermons, along with a series of the saddest and most depressing songs, were deliberately avoided. The goal was to revive the family for the future. Life must and will move on, whether we are with it or not. My father would have wanted it no other way.

Another part of my responsibilities included monitoring, supervising, and investing the remainder of his total estate after all funeral expenses. His will also specified that his wife, Lela, be given the opportunity to claim and if she desired, consume all of his funds. She requested and was given full control of his funds. I did not charge a fee for handling my father's estate.

One of the most astounding experiences of my life occurred the day I met Mr. Brice for the first time. He owned a business establishment at Woodard and Blackstock, South Carolina. My father, who was illiterate and could not write his name, loved and trusted Mr. Brice with his total life savings. They had transacted business together for more than 45 years. Mr. Brice was trusted by my father more than any other member in his immediate family. It was an example of a perfect bond between two human beings.

I walked up to Mr. Brice, introduced myself as Lemmon Stevenson, the son of Dan Stevenson. I further stated, "My father is in the Columbia Veterans Hospital dying from cancer. He has already made a will and appointed me executor of his estate. He also asked me to collect from you all of his money. Attorney McDonald, my Daddy, and I have developed a detailed plan for utilizing all of his savings."

Mr. Brice gave me one of those startling looks and yelled, "Who are you? Where did you come from? Dan don't have any sons. Dan never told me anything about you! I didn't know he had a son. I am not about to give Dan's money to you or anybody else! He has trusted me with his money and I shall <u>never</u> betray that trust."

Although many so-called friends of my father had accused Mr. Brice of being a crook, evil, and selfish, I immediately gained a tremendous amount of respect for him as a human. That respect grew even wider as we reviewed the records he kept on my Daddy's money. He finally turned all of the money over to me. We shook hands and he stated that, "You must have been God-sent."

Chapter Fourteen

Family

L ife is no respecter of person. It does not care about your race, gender or nationality. It offers no quotas or affirmative action to anyone, and it could care less about whether you are rich or poor. In the end, the playing field is level and everyone pays the piper. Fortunately, there has always been and there will always be a positive side. It is the responsibility of each and everyone of us to use our eyes and ears to see and hear the positive and constructive message of life.

)()()()()(

Everywhere I have gone in recent years, people are asking me about my wife. What is she like? How and where did you meet her, and how long have you two been married?

I met my wife, Cecile Ross Stevenson, in October 1943, during a fall stroll down Main Street in Winnsboro, South Carolina. She was with two other girls and I was accompanied by two other boys. The other girls and guys knew each other and they had been close friends for several months. Cecile and I introduced ourselves to each other and talked in general about everything, including the weather.

She was streamlined with very long curly black hair and the most gorgeous smile I had ever seen. She was extremely nice, courteous, and receptive. I really enjoyed talking with her and felt very comfortable until I asked her about grade classification. I found out that she was a ninth grader and was the daughter of our high school principal, Professor W. A. Ross, Sr. Her mother, Mrs. Beatrice Ross, was a primary teacher in the same school through twelfth grade at Fairfield County Training School. I was a seventh grader in the same school. My self-confidence and degree of self-worth tumbled immediately to zero and below.

In order to understand and fully appreciate the above sentence, it is necessary to understand the hierarchy of high class society within the black communities at that time. Many well-educated and apparently economically secure black families were racist, snobbish, and downright oppressive to other poor and less fortunate blacks. I simply did not feel worthy of having a high school principal's daughter as my girlfriend.

Cecile had three older brothers and two older sisters. They were all very professional people. Her oldest brother, Dr. William A. Ross, Jr., was a medical doctor in Jefferson City, Missouri. He was highly respected, a shrewd businessman, a civil rights leader, and a staunch promoter of educational opportunities for young people. In August 1996, Dr. Ross suprised everyone by announcing a $400,000 scholarship fund which he had established for desendents of Beatrice and William Ross, Sr. He firmly believes in the power of education and the profound need for its growth and development in every human being.

Her second oldest brother was a very outstanding Presbyterian minister and missionary director. Her next oldest brother was a contractor and a master brick mason. Her oldest sister was a professional musician, English teacher, and director of several choirs in the area. She was, without question, the most beautiful human I have ever seen. She was very nice and was the wife of perhaps the richest black man in South Carolina. Her next oldest sister was a school teacher, school principal, and superintendent of schools. Her father, compared to other black educators in the state, simply had no equals.

At that particular point in time, I had one or maybe two girls who had shown some interest in me. Cecile also had one or two boyfriends. However, she would always smile and talk briefly with me on regular occasions. I thought she was just being nice until one day we were talking and three of her snobbish friends came by and said, as loud as they could, "Cecile, why are you wasting your time with him? Lemmon is a nobody. You deserve better."

She put her arms upon my shoulders and continued talking and smiling as if she did not see or hear them. Several months later I asked her why she was willing to spend time with me. Her answer was because I love you.

My adopted mother, Ella, found out about the other girl who I felt comfortable talking with because she was on the same social level as myself. Ella became outrageously upset and hostile about my association with the other girl. She said that she knew the girl's mother and total family and felt that it was not a suitable family for me. About 12 or 16 months later, Ella found out that I was courting Cecile, the principal's daughter. She became so upset over my association with Cecile that I thought she was going have a heart attack. She told me that I did not have any money or education and my family was too poor to be associated with the professor's family. "Even if that girl does like you, her family will not tolerate it."

Susan Stevenson-Stewart,
"Matriarch and the essence
of faith."

Ester Boyd-Stevenson,
(Lemmon's mother) with
his sister, Nancy, and
brother, Walter.

Henretta and Ella Stewart

*Professor William A. Ross, Sr.,
Headmaster, Fairfield
County Training School.*

*Lemmon's father,
Dan Stevenson.*

Lemmon's oldest daughter and
her family—Anita Stevenson-
Gathers, Jerome Gathers,
Jerome, Jr., Brian and
Tiffany.

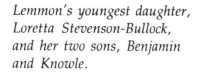

Lemmon's youngest daughter,
Loretta Stevenson-Bullock,
and her two sons, Benjamin
and Knowle.

Mrs. Cecile Stevenson

Lemmon's daughter, Donna Stevenson reigning as Miss Homecoming Queen at South Carolina State University with President Maceo Nance.

Dr. William A. Ross, Jr.
Founder of the scholarship fund
for desendents of Beatrice and
William A. Ross, Sr.

Lemmon and his
"Big M" in 1958.

Lemmon, Cecile and children, 1967.
(Left to right: Lemmon, Jr., Anita, Loretta, Donna, and Joseph)

At this point, I was convinced that no girl would be acceptable to my mother. The other girl was too poor and her family was too bad for me. Cecile's family was too rich and too highly educated for me. I was really upset when I found out that my mother was sneaking into my trunk and reading my love letters. I decided to go with whomever I pleased and that I would keep my family out of my social life.

When I was a high school senior and Cecile was a college student, I took Cecile to visit my parents. My mother was so impressed with Cecile that she had a private conference with her in which she told Cecile all of my weaknesses and faults that she could think of. I simply could not believe that my mother would do such a terrible thing to her only son. She told Cecile that I was selfish, stubborn, bullheaded, greedy, and that nobody could ever tell me anything to change my mind once it had been made up. She told Cecile a whole lot more than that but I'm not about to repeat it in this book. My mother's actions made me mad, but my mother didn't care. She loved Cecile. That love relationship between my mother and Cecile continued until my mother passed away. Cecile simply could never do anything wrong.

In 1952, two weeks after I graduated from college, I took Cecile and her mother and father to meet my family. My mother was shocked to find out that the Ross family was not snobbish, or uppity, and did not appear to feel that they were better than other common black people. Cecile and I had already decided to get married, and on August 2, 1952, we "tied the knot." Love knows no respecter of person and when the lovebug strikes, you will have been had. It matters not the social class, economic condition, race, or nationality.

Neither one of us had any money of our own but we

agreed to live separately, independently, and apart from both families. Cecile had been a school teacher for two years prior to our marriage. We rented an apartment in Chester, South Carolina, which is about 25 miles north of Winnsboro, South Carolina.

One truly amazing and exciting experience occurred. During a state teachers' convention in Columbia, South Carolina, it was my good fortune to have my father-in-law introduce me to my former seventh grade teacher as his son-in-law. She was the teacher who told me that I was nothing and would always be nothing. I was a science teacher in the Fenley Senior High School, located in the city of Chester, South Carolina. This teacher, whom we had named "witch," stood there with her mouth open in startling amazement. She simply could not accept what she was seeing and hearing. The whole thing was sweet music to my eyes and ears. The only regret that I can think of is that we did not have a movie camera to catch her facial expression.

In November 1952, I was drafted into the United States Army and was stationed in France for 18 months. I had the good fortune to travel all over Europe. My wife was busy traveling back and forth between our two families. Our first child was born in June 1953. We were all very excited about his arrival, and I simply could not wait to get home to see him. Cecile wrote me on a regular basis and she would always send pictures of our son.

Cecile was and still is the best possible mother for our five children and nine grandchildren. Being a full-time mother and, at the same time, serving as a full-time teacher in the Greenville School District and later in the Boyertown School District is a perfect example of "mission impossible." Miraculously, Cecile handled the whole situation in the most graceful and dignified manner imaginable. Also, having a high school principal and a full-time classroom teacher for parents have not been easy for our children.

Endeavoring to please their parents, friends, teachers, and be accepted and appreciated by peers could never happen. There is no known way to please everybody, and the notion of being fully accepted and appreciated by others is a reality that even Jesus Christ and all the prophets and saints of the Bible were unable to accomplish. The names and occupations of our five children are: Lemmon Albert, a chemical technician with two children; Joseph, a home improvement worker and a musician with one child; Anita, a pharmacist with three children; Donna Jean, an engineer with one child; and Loretta, an office manager with two children.

I had three brothers and one sister. Their names and locations are Nancy Stevenson Harrison, Hartford, Connecticut; Walter Stevenson, Buffalo, New York; Robert Stevenson, Winnsboro, South Carolina; and Charlie Stevenson, Baltimore, Maryland. All of my brothers have died. However, they have all enriched me with a large number of nieces and nephews. I also have one adopted sister from my adopted Stewart family. Her name is Henretta Stewart, and she is still living in Winnsboro, South Carolina.

Cecile has always been a firm, stern, and a no-nonsense disciplinarian with all our children. However, with the arrival of our nine grandchildren, there has been a total breakdown in her discipline practices. She loves those grandchildren so much that they can never do anything wrong. The degree to which she has spoiled her grandchildren is unbelievable.

Chapter Fifteen

The Gambling Reality of Life

I n spite of all the hundreds of fire and brimstone sermons I have heard pertaining to the sinfulness, evil, and total condemnation of gambling, the whole world operates on the theory of probability—maybe yes or maybe no. Life offers absolutely no guarantees to anyone, and there is almost nothing in this world for which we can be absolutely certain. The contention that life is a gamble and that it is saturated with risks and uncertainties, from the cradle to the grave, is an indisputable truism.

)()()()()(

When I completed all requirements for the Masters of Education Degree from South Carolina State College, I was certain of my continuous ignorance and the impelling need for continued educational growth and development. Initially, I did not feel qualified to attend South Carolina State College. However, I gambled and won. I knew, beyond a reasonable doubt, that I was not qualified and that I would probably never be qualified to compete favorably with those gifted white students at the University of Missouri.

Regardless of my perceived inadequacies, I was willing to

gamble away my safe and secure principalship at the Mitford School with the hope and belief that I would surely be successful and no doubt get a better job. Again, I gambled and won. I definitely got what I needed and desired most—a superior education. I am ready and fully prepared to compete as an effective educator with any individual or group of individuals anywhere in the world.

I owe all of this courage, self-esteem, and confidence to several South Carolina State and University of Missouri professors and administrators who demonstrated sufficient humanitarian and courageous professional qualities necessary to accept me and provide solid and unwavering support for me, not as a black man, but as another human being struggling to achieve the best possible education in order that it could be shared with all children, regardless of race, throughout this nation. No degree of success on my part could have occurred at the University of Missouri without their help. I was told that I would have to "earn my own place in the sun" but they would guarantee me equality of educational opportunity during the teaching and learning processes at the University of Missouri.

I did not receive another academic degree from the University of Missouri, but I did get certification as a high school principal, superintendent, and also an "A" professional certificate from the State of South Carolina. I was already certified as an elementary teacher and elementary principal with a "B" professional certificate.

My Mitford School principalship paid $2,000 per year. Following my resignation of Mitford School, I was recruited by the Great Falls School District to serve as principal of Elizabeth Heights Elementary and Senior High School, grades 1 through 12. The significance of this particular promotion included a salary increase up to $6,500. Most importantly, Elizabeth Heights High School was the school attended by most of Mitford's graduates and it allowed me the opportunity to continue to work with many of the Mitford students and parents.

It was an extreme rarity for the Mitford Great Fall Community students to finish high school. Going to or finishing college was basically unthinkable. My principalship, along with the solid support of the superintendent, school board, parents, students, and community, Elizabeth Heights' graduates were guaranteed a four year college scholarship if they would dare show determination and commitment to hard work and the determination to earn an education.

The perceived difficulties involved in administering the Elizabeth Heights High School had motivated two of its previous principals to retire or seek employment elsewhere. The school had lost its accreditation and the school community was in complete chaos. We organized, developed, implemented, and evaluated a program that restored the school's accreditation in one year. We also restored community pride in the school, along with profound support and mutual respect for the rights and responsibilities of others.

This represents another example of my gambling with love and service over hate, greed, and defendable excuses. We gambled everything on love, respect, honor, self-pride, responsibility, and equality of educational opportunity and won. The legacy of pride and honor of Elizabeth Heights graduates is stronger than every before.

I know of no school system in the southeast that is more highly prestigious, respected, industrially developed, and financially stable than the Greenville School District, which is located in Greenville, South Carolina. It had more than 100 schools in 1965. As the principal of Joseph E. Beck High School, I operated one of the most innovative and prestigious school in Greenville history. I was also offered a promotion to serve as program developer for the total school district. I simply cannot find words to fully explain the pain and suffering I experienced by turning down this honorable and truly exciting offer. Not only do I love educational program development, but I am a very good developer.

For better or worse, I voluntarily gambled away my professional employment future with the Greenville District by resigning and moving my family to Pottstown, Pennsylvania. This move turned out to be a big win, and it was also a big loss for me. It was a superior win because my three daughters were exposed to the most challenging educational opportunities this nation has to offer. Much of their high school training and preparedness was on the college or university level. They enjoyed the guidance, counsel, invigorating and inspiring teaching from one of the most outstanding high school faculties to be found anywhere in the world.

Lives of great men and women remind us that this world is and always has been saturated with shattered dreams. No one ever gets exactly what he wants when he wants it, and the exact conditions under which he wants it. As my wife constantly reminds me, into each life some rain will fall and some days will be dark, dreary, and disappointing. However, we must always keep hope alive, never give up, and keep traveling on.

One of the most exciting experiences of my life is that most hardships, roadblocks, and disappointments experienced by me have been turned into profound successes and achievements far superior to anything I have ever imagined. History tells us that any human being has the capacity to transform his/her liabilities into meaningful and honorable assets.

Chapter Sixteen

Education

*A*ny nation expecting to be free, half educated and half ignorant, is expecting what never was and never will be. Education is America's only hope for freedom, survival and productivity. Therefore, this country, beginning at the national level and extending down through the states, counties and hamlets, must declare war on ignorance and ensure its destruction by whatever means necessary.

)()()()()(

Because of my lifelong service in the field of education, several of my associates suggested that I should state some of my personal ideas, beliefs, and convictions concerning education. Therefore, I have decided to address this issue by raising and answering three questions: What is education? Where did it come from? And, where should it be going?

Education is life. It begins at birth, and it is continuous, non-stop until death do we part. There is no human in the whole world who is fully educated. There is always something else to be discovered, utilized, learned, appreciated, or preserved. Perhaps the biggest myth that has developed in the minds of too many human beings is that when you finish high school, college, and certainly when you earn the Ph.D. Degree, you will have arrived. Sorry. I have news for you. You will have only reached a new beginning. The truth of this reality would not change if you had the good fortune of earning several Ph.D.'s.

I am not suggesting that we should not earn Ph.D. Degrees. I am convinced, beyond a reasonable doubt, that we should acquire as much education as we possibly can and that we should definitely earn as many advanced academic degrees as we possibly can. I was working toward a Ph.D., and I believe I would have eventually earned one. However, my priorities changed. I had to go to work and earn money to support my family. I had a wife and five children to support, and I was flat broke.

The bottom line here is to make sure we place advanced academic degrees in proper context. There is always something else to learn and something else to do. Although there are private and public school opportunities available to children and adults of America, some of the most highly successful, educated, and financially independent people have not earned a high school diploma. The formal education we receive from school is only part of the process.

Sometimes I think of education as a process through which we grow continuously from the cradle to the grave. Modern technology, such as radio, television, and computers, can help any human learn how to read. If we learn how to read and would dare read some of everything we are able to secure, we will be able to learn and do anything we set our minds to.

My main contention is and always has been earning an education through the public schools. My research on the origin of public education goes back to the 1800's. Horace Mann has been labeled as the Father of Education through the free public school. The story is alleged that on one occasion Horace Mann encountered one of his opponents who contended that the Lock Step

Graded School was wrong, unrealistic, and unacceptable. Mann is reported to have replied, "Who are you to criticize my structured school system? What have you done? What school structure have you developed that is equal to or superior to my system? Until you develop a system superior to mine, I have absolutely nothing more to say to you!"

Horace Mann's public school structure was established at Lexington (now Framingham), Massachusetts, in 1839. It is now 1997, a total of 158 years. It appears to me that if Mann's public school structure was so lousy, someone out of the thousands of outstanding educators of this nation would have been able to establish a superior replacement system for Mann's graded school structure.

Public school education as we know it today came from Framingham, Massachusetts, in 1839. We did not do a satisfactory job of writing in the public schools during the 1800's, and we are not doing a satisfactory job during the 1900's. However, I do believe some improvements are being made. Arithmetic (math) is good in the 1990's and it was also good in the 1800's. Continuous non-stop drills and reinforcement in reading and math was practiced in the 1800's and the same thing is true in the 1900's. In fact, I know of no other assured method of mastering basic skills other than repetition and constant reinforcement. The more we read, the better we will be able to read. The more we write, the better we will be able to write.

Our current and future reading and language programs should definitely utilize the whole language approach. Using whole, non-censored, authentic pieces of literature is the most meaningful and effective method of meeting the reading needs of all students, kindergarten through eighth grade. Whole language material is so interesting that students will be naturally motivated to read.

I have had the opportunity to study, work with, and evaluate the graded school structure and also the non-graded school structure. As a result, I am convinced that it makes absolutely no difference what system is used because good teachers will excel in the graded school structure and good teachers will also excel in the non-graded system. Good principals are just as effective with the graded school system as they are with the non-graded system. Money is and has always been a problem in education.

I conducted a non-graded school including Grades 1 through 8 in South Carolina in 1955. We combined first and second grades because we did not have enough classrooms and teachers to separate the two classes. We merged Grades 3, 4, and 5 because we did not have sufficient classrooms and staff to isolate these grades. We also combined Grades 6, 7, and 8 in the same manner. It was most encouraging and exciting to see our first grade students learn how to read and then actually outperform second graders. We had a similarly large number of third graders who outperformed fifth graders. I also remember bringing some third graders into the seventh and eighth grade group. The third grade students sometimes embarrassed eighth graders to the superlative degree, and they had fun doing it. Some of our students were of the opinion that third graders were smarter than eigth graders.

Unfortunately, we are experiencing a breakdown in student discipline, responsibility, respect, and appreciation for hard work and self-esteem, or individual self-worth. I think we are going to have to do whatever is necessary to get those principles back into our schools. Discipline is the number one problem. Self-discipline and control is the key ingredient for success, not only in a school teaching and learning situation, but in any meaningful or honorable goal. I am convinced that student rights and freedom without discipline and responsibility guarantees chaos.

Thurgood Marshall, Martin Luther King, Malcolm X, and

other famous civil rights leaders did a wonderful job providing freedom for black and white citizens of this country. However, there was one little ingredient missing and that was responsibility. In order for freedom to have any real meaning, we must *produce four pounds of responsibility for every one pound of freedom.* I have told my students on several occasions that they have the constitutional right to be ignorant, backward, stupid, and lazy. They do not have the right, however, to interfere with others who are trying to learn.

Therefore, I have never hesitated to remove from the senior high, junior high, middle, and elementary school any child regardless of race or economic status who interferes with or disrupts the learning process of other students. Students who interfere with other students who are trying to learn or disrupt the educational process must be suspended, not only from the classroom but from the total school environment. This weird notion of in-school suspension is the most insane, cowardly, and irresponsible cop-out approach to discipline imaginable.

For maximum success and effectiveness, it is essential for our schools to have student, parent, and community involvement. Also, the tax supported public school system was designed to serve and meet the individual needs of children, not superintendents, boards of education, principals, teachers, and politicians. Pertaining to the above contention, most school district budgets are excessive and slanted in the wrong direction. Specifically, the school district budget must be lean and uncompromisingly mean toward any and everything that is not of direct benefit to our children of Grades K through 12. Our students are the best and they deserve the best possible training because they are the only future this nation has.

Most importantly, parents have the right, obligation, and profound responsibility to be involved in the total teaching and learning process of their children. Parents must be fully aware of what the school is doing to educate their children, why it is doing what it does, and how parents can be helpful in ensuring the success of the school's plan. At a minimum, every public school principal should send out a survey form to all parents living in the school's attendance area. The survey should include at least the following three questions: What do you like best about your school? What do you like least about your school? What do you think we should do together to correct perceived school problems?

If there are parents and citizens who feel that they are not qualified to participate in the educational process of their children, they probably don't realize that at least 85% of all the problems involved in educating our young people can be corrected with common sense. Reference here is made to plain old horse sense. No professor, board member, superintendent, principal, or teacher, regardless of the number of earned academic degrees, has a monopoly on common sense. Lack of it is definitely our number one problem in education.

I would also suggest to public school board members, superintendents, principals, and teachers who are hopeful of improving the quality of education in their school systems by constantly raising property taxes and begging for state and national financing, that without a solid, safe, disciplined learning atmosphere, you are expecting what never was and never will be! This is especially true of inner city school districts.

Constant demands for more money is not the answer. All major industries throughout this nation and the world are downsizing and demanding more for less. Why should public school systems be allowed to be the exact opposite? The voucher system and other major organizational changes are certain to occur should this unlimited property taxation madness continue. Also, as much as I have hated and resented the bell curve and standardized testing, I am now convinced that all students, regardless of race, should and must be taught and conditioned to compete on standardized tests favorable with all other students of this nation and the world.

The physical condition of our young people is deteriorating to an all-time low, and it represents a process that has been gradual and continuous since the 1800's. During the 1800's, most of us lived on farms and physical conditioning was a natural process. Since that period of time, most of us are cooped up in high rise city apartments, other rentals, or privately owned homes. Accordingly, health and physical education for all public school children should be priority one. The statement, *when you have got your health, you have got just about everything,* is the indisputable truth. A strong, invigorating physical education program coupled with a highly nutritious lunch program is a must. Hungry children do not and cannot learn well.

Reading, writing, and arithmetic (math) is the next priority area. This area must be supplemented and reinforced with science, vocational education, history, radio, television, languages, and computer technology. Our young people must be trained and conditioned to compete academically with all other children of this nation and the world. Also, the common virtues of truth, honesty, justice, integrity, courtesy, courage, perseverance, hard work, and responsibility are just as important as hard core academic or intellectual training. There is nothing in all the world that is more important than to help condition our young people to become good, responsible citizens. Hate, greed, and violence are destroying our young and older citizens by the thousands. Accordingly, it is the duty and responsibility of each and everyone of us to do whatever is necessary to reverse this unacceptable problem.

Chapter Seventeen

The Expensive Reality of Effective School Administration

T hroughout this book, I have endeavored to highlight the reality that everyone pays the piper. Life is no respecter of person and sooner or later everyone will pay! You may run but you cannot hide. Life has your number, and she knows where you live. You may run on for a long time, but sooner or later, life will definitely cut you down. The cue here is to pay your dues up front by selecting and preparing for a profession that you would be willing to die for if necessary. It has been said, and I agree, that the individual who cannot or will not find a mission in life worthy of dying for is not fitting to live.

)()()()()()(

Mr. Albert Richburg, my Assistant Principal, and I spent four years in college and another three years in graduate school, preparing for the principalship at intercity Beck High School. We worked day and night to make Beck the best possible educational center for young people. We were severely criticized, humiliated, and even threatened by some people who did not like our firm, unflexible and uncompromising discipline policies and the fact that we required our students to work continuously to the limit of their mental and physical abilities. We literally placed our lives on the line, day and night, for five years.

Every occupation, profession, or enterprise is saturated with challenges, hardships, phonies, deceit, fraud, injustices, greedy freeloaders, thieves, and "scumbags." Although the legal profession and national politics are believed to lead the pack, the educational profession is no exception.

The proper question here is why anybody in their right mind would want a career in the teaching profession? We all know that it is truly a "mission impossible" and the financial rewards for a lifetime of service would make it impossible for you to become rich.

My answer to this question is based on two factors. The first one is point-in-time. During the 1940's and 50's, the only professional jobs available to black people were primarily teaching or preaching. Since I could no longer tolerate the fire and brimstone rhetoric of the preaching profession, I willingly, graciously, and excitedly chose the teaching profession.

The other factor is that I am a product of the American public school system, beginning in first grade and continuing through the eleventh grade. I know firsthand what the system was like, and I learned how to hate it with a passion. Most importantly, when I found out that hating and criticizing the school system would not make it better, I paid the supreme price of becoming a part of the system that had to be changed and actually started the changing process. My efforts have been continuous since 1952. I am fully aware of those who will say: Who are you and what have you done to make things better in education? It is not what I have done, but rather what I have been able to get others to do that has made the difference. Also, the writing of this book is my way of making sure that the current and future generations of young people will have the opportunity to read at least one true story of public education and what we must do to make it better.

One of these bitter weeds that I despise the most is deceit. Why can't we just face our problems and opponents up-front, face-to-face, and head-on. These pampering, procrastinating and cover-up schemes are truly sickening. I am reminded of my first principalship at the Mitford School located in South Carolina. My teachers were old enough to be my mother. Many of them were old enough to be my grandmother. They would all come up to me and say, "Mr. Stevenson, you are a fine man and a very good principal, and we are so very proud of you." The minute my back was turned, the same people would say, "Devil! Devil! Devil! He is just Satan. We must do everything we can to get rid of him."

The very next day, that same group of teachers would invite my wife and me to dinner at their homes. They would serve us the most elaborate dinners money could buy. However, the back-biting and verbal deceptions continued. How did I handle this deceit? I learned how to cover up and pretend that it did not exist. Our mission was to meet the educational needs of children and my teachers were highly dedicated and effective in accomplishing this mission. We organized, developed and implemented the best professional program for our students. If any teacher knew of a better plan than the one we used, it would definitely be considered.

However, any teacher who abused a child, refused to implement or follow agreed upon procedures, were fired immediately—no questions asked. I remember saying to one teacher, "If you think that I am going to recommend that you get paid to abuse our students and not help meet their educational needs, you are nuts!"

I remember saying to my superintendent, "The only way this teacher will be able to continue working in this school will be for you to make her principal and dismiss me. The choice is yours." There is another side. I do not recall ever firing a teacher who loved children and would do whatever she could to help them learn and to feel worthy as human beings. I would hold onto them no matter what they said or did to me. In South Carolina and in Pennsylvania, I have had teachers say and do some very compelling things. Truly professional teachers are not interested in pleasing the boss or worrying about whether or not they will gain financially. They are primarily concerned about doing what's in the best interest of the children.

One example was a teacher who did not like proposed changes to a special educational program of which she was in charge. Rather than just knuckling under, she made it clear to me that she did not like the changes and would resign if they were made. In her heart, she felt that the changes would not be in the best interest of the students and prepared a letter of resignation because she felt that after her verbal outburst, I would fire her.

This teacher represented the courage, commitment and skills that were essential for the success of our program. I remember tearing up her letter and making her chairman of the special program in question. I told her that if I could ever do anything to help her, she should not hesitate to demand whatever was needed. We became true professional partners and ignorance in our school was in big, big trouble!

Another unethical and totally unacceptable bitter weed is theft. All of the supplies and materials for the operation of the Beck School had to be purchased with student fees. Half of the Beck Students could not afford student fees. Therefore, we conducted colossal fund raisers. Other schools in the district and state conducted fund raisers. Unfortunately, I have heard several principals actually brag about how they used school funds illegally for their personal benefit. I simply cannot understand how any teacher or principal could stoop so low as to rob his school's students of their educational benefits. Principals should set examples for their professional staff by announcing publicly, ahead of time, the specific projects for which money will be raised. They should establish a fund raising committee, and make absolutely certain that he does not touch one penny of the money raised.

Perhaps the two greatest sins in education are social promotion and the academic freedom of choice available to students. Currently, our students do have the choice of becoming educated or remaining dumb, stupid, ignorant, and irresponsible. This freedom of choice practiced has been a disaster for many students—nationwide. This practice must be eliminated. We should require all students to succeed academically to the limit of their abilities in a regular school environment or they should be required to succeed academically in a special boot camp arrangement for unruly, disruptive, and irresponsible students. Under no circumstances should any student be allowed to graduate from any school before demonstrating mastery of minimal academic requirements.

Occasionally, I am inclined to agree with the old familiar saying that, "God must have loved poor, weak, ignorant, underprivileged, and severely disadvantaged human beings, because he made so many of them." Also, in spite of the aggressive, demanding, and most extensive civil rights movement, beginning in 1863, when Abraham Lincoln signed the Emancipation Proclamation and ending in 1997 with Franklin D. Roosevelt, Lyndon B. Johnson, and U.S. Supreme Court Justice, Earl Warren's welfare, the great society affirmative action programs, and the desegregation of our public schools, over 50% of this nation's citizens are ignorant, poor, and severely disadvantaged.

In reality, we are talking about more than 137 years of government sponsored relief and support for its citizens. Even though these services have been helpful to thousands of individuals of all races in America, they are flawed and ineffective to the extent that it is impossible for our government to do for its citizens the things that its citizens can and should do for themselves. What is the answer? Individual selected and sponsored programs which places health, education, responsibility, and total commitment to hard work and perseverance necessary for self-sufficiency in our free society.

Our educational programs, beginning with four year old kindergarten, must be so inspiring, exciting and challenging that our elementary children will be ashamed to goof off and not assume responsibility for their self-discipline and learning. The government never has and never will be able to do for us what we can and should do for ourselves. The wisdom of our elders declares, upon a stack of Bibles, that if we could dare chastise, discipline, and raise our children in the proper direction, when they are older, they will not depart from it. This is not just a good way to raise children—it is the only responsible, effective, and respectable way!

Chapter Eighteen

Religion

There is absolutely no question in my mind about the existence of a Supreme Commander or ruler of the universe. There is no way in the world for all of these past and current miracles to have occurred by chance. Now, the name or the label others place on the Supreme Ruler is irrelevant to me. However, I have chosen to call Him God and Ruler of the Universe. The rules, guidelines, and operating procedures of our Divine Ruler are documented in the entire Bible, Genesis through Revelation.

I like the New Testament and Jesus Christ, the despised one, the so-called troublemaker, the nonconformist who declared that all things are possible if we would only read and study the "Word," believe the "Word," and have the courage, conviction, and determination to put the "Word" into practice. In other words, we must be doers and not hearers only. Jesus was a man of action, and He got things done. Christianity, as we now know it, was one of His major achievements.

I like Jesus because He did not allow anything or anybody to stop or prevent Him from doing or accomplishing anything He set out to accomplish. His past words were courage and perseverance. Although He was rejected by His home community and so-called friends, was not famous, had no money, and was the most hated and despised person of all the world, He is still, after a huge number of centuries, the most famous and highest respected central figure of the human race.

)()()()()(

I was born and raised in the Methodist Church and changed over to the Baptist Church after becoming an adult. As an educator in the public school system of this nation, I have been confronted with the "separation of church and school" mentality. Mainly, it is concerned with the mixing of education and religion. Religion is of man and when I think of the destructive disaster man has made of religion, I am the first to say that the process of educating our young people in the public schools and religion should never be allowed to mix, under any circumstances.

However, God, Christianity, and church, as revealed in the Bible, is not separated from anything or anybody. Wherever we go and whatever we do, God is there. He is profoundly embedded in the heart, mind, and soul of every living creature. God creates and makes available to every human being a natural spirituality that is of sufficient strength and power to see anyone, regardless of race, nationality, or gender, through any problem, trouble, crisis or disaster, including death. Most importantly, this spirituality is free for the asking. All you have to do is just tune in to it. Also, in cases of emergencies, you will not even have to tune in. God will tune for you automatically. You will need no money, you will not need parent, teacher, or minister permission and in fact, you will not even have to belong to a church. Most of God's business and work here on earth has nothing to do with church.

I have already mentioned my involvement with the Methodist and Baptist churches. Also, please know that I would take nothing in exchange for this educational experience. One of the most important things I learned concerning my church involvement was that in spite of all the devils, hypocrites, and phonies to be found in our churches, the church represents the best people and the best God has to offer to others, especially strangers.

Therefore, every time I find myself in a new or strange place, I always go to the church. God and His church have never let me down. When I was an elementary principal in Winnsboro, South Carolina, God and His church were there. God and His church were also present when I became a high school principal in Great Falls, South Carolina. I really needed God and His church when I became high school principal in the city of Greenville, South Carolina. As a lost and misplaced South Carolinian in Pottstown, Pennsylvania, I perceived God and His church as a welcomed friend.

In closing this unit, I would like to suggest to our Sunday school teachers, deacons, and ministers that it would be helpful if we concentrated on a balance of the Bible rather than narrow, isolated sections. The God I know, love, honor, and serve is much more than this notion of slamblasting and condemning everything and everybody to hell. Also, I am convinced beyond a reasonable doubt that "we should prepare for over yonder," but I am also convinced that we should prepare for "over here." God's work here on earth must be done by man. Accordingly, if we will do the very best job we possibly can to help make this world a better place in which to live, while we are alive and well, we will not have to worry about dying and going "over yonder."

Chapter Nineteen

Looking Backward and Forward

T he adventurous journey of life, from the cradle to the grave, for any human being, national or international, can be phenomenal. There are jobs to be done, loads to lift, wrongs to be corrected, illness to be cured, poverty and ignorance to overcome, freedom to be won and maintained, and injustices to be corrected, oppressions to be removed, young people to be motivated, inspired, and led. Most importantly, we have the American Dream to be understood, pursued, and preserved. We also have the Word of God and Christianity to help us understand and resolve the problems of religion which have been created by man.

However, having traveled this adventurous journey for more than 69 years, this writer finds it extremely difficult if not impossible to understand how any real red-blooded American can ever find life boring. How in the world could anyone be so blind as to miss the positive and constructive excitement of life? Also, the period of time in which we live really does not matter. It has been said and I fully agree that "All times are good times if we but know what do with them."

Looking back on my life and the lives of many of my associates, there is and apparently always has been key professional and intellectually brilliant individuals available and ready to assist anyone who is daring enough to tackle any major humanitarian cause. It is also important to be aware of the need to think and act big. The larger and more impossible the goal, the greater and more profound will be the assistance and support.

God supports and sustains His own. All you have to do is move into decisive, deliberate, responsible, and aggressive action. "You make one step, and I will make two," is a Christian legacy that has followed me since childhood. Also, "All things, good and evil, work together for the good of those who love God." I desired, wanted, and was able to get an excellent education. No evil public school teacher, college professor, or university professor was able to stop me. In reality, their opposition to me served as a natural motivator which has helped guarantee my success.

When my wife and I decided to build our first dream home, there was this question of credit. No bank in the State of South Carolina would dare loan us sufficient funds to pay the construction costs. We had no money, no credit rating, and our incomes were so low that no mainstream lending agency would dare take a chance with us. We reviewed several truly gorgeous house plans, selected the one we liked best, and actually started the building process.

We dug and finished the foundation with our emergency funds. We cut and used our own lumber, purchased sufficient concrete blocks and bricks along with necessary roofing materials to completely frame, complete the brick work, and cover the home. We also purchased windows and doors. From the outside, our home looked as if it were finished. Several of our startled associates made the comment, "Anyone who has the audacity to dig the foundation just might finish the home."

I qualified for a veteran's loan, but I was unable to get any state agency to sponsor me. One fee-greedy lawyer suggested that we try to get a direct loan from the Federal Government. He agreed to represent me for an outrageous fee. However, he assured us that there were no guarantees that the loan would ever be approved. We immediately rejected his offer. Fortunately, an all black life insurance company known as North Carolina Mutual heard of our troubles and delivered us out of our home financing problems. It also allowed us to build a credit rating.

When I found myself lost and a total misfit at the University of Missouri, one dean and three truly outstanding professors combined their efforts and made absolutely certain that I receive every possible chance to succeed. The Head of the Department of Education received extensive pressures from other professors and staff to dismiss me from the university. Their main contention was that I was not qualified and should not have ever been admitted. My score on the university required test, Miller Analogy, was incredibly low.

Dean Townsend; Professor W. W. Carpenter, Director of State and National Educational Administration; Dr. Lois Knowles, Professor of Elementary Education; and Dr. A. Stern Artley, Professor and Head of the Reading Department, University of Missouri and Senior Author for Scott-Foresman Publishing Company arranged for me to remain at the University of Missouri for four summers and one full academic year.

When two highly influential professors suggested that I be required to do a special problem to determine my qualifications to remain at the university, I received several suggestions on how to do my written project report. The school required me to do a written project on pupil personnel services and also take a course in that area. I received an "A" on the written report and also an "A" in the college graduate course. I also voluntarily did a project on standardized psychological testing at Mitford School in Winnsboro, South Carolina.

When our family medical doctor, Dr. Floyd, found out that we were leaving Greenville, South Carolina, and moving to Pottstown, Pennsylvania, he was gravely concerned about our future welfare. On one occasion he stated to me, "Lemmon, I simply cannot understand why anyone in his right mind would want to leave Greenville, South Carolina, and go to Pennsylvania. You are going to be lost up there."

What Dr. Floyd did not know and I did not bother to tell him was that we were lost when we moved to Greenville. Dr. M. T. Anderson, County School Superintendent, Mr. Fred L. Fowler, City School Superintendent, Mr. Thomas Kerns, Sterling High School Teacher and Housing Developer, provided my wife and me with everything we needed to get started. Also, when we moved to Pottstown, Pennsylvania, Dr. Ray E. Feick, Superintendent of Schools, Mr. Anthony Zampella, High School Principal, Mrs. Dorothy Schmearer, Primary Teacher, and Mr. John Foster, Chemical Company Supervisor and spokesman for the Community Coordinating Committee, Mrs. Catherine Beasely, community activist, helped my wife and me considerably.

When we arrived in Pottstown, I had already developed a tentative plan for the operation of the Jefferson School. I remember explaining to the Jefferson staff that I have never attempted to do anything without a bona fide plan. After reviewing the plan with staff, I also informed them that if anyone had any concerns about the plan or if anyone had or knew of a better plan to meet the educational needs of the Jefferson School, I would be delighted to consider it. If not, everyone was expected to follow and support my plan to the fullest possible extent.

The plan was revised and updated on a regular basis. With input from staff and community, it became **our** plan rather than my plan. When our updated plan called for computers and closed-circuit televisions, and there was no district budget to cover the costs, financial support came from Sunset Pharmacy, Super Fresh Food Market, the Pennsylvania State Department of Education, the U.S. Office of Education, the Cabot Corporation located in Boyertown, and colossal fund raisers by parents, students, and community.

When my program became our program, the staff and parents would not hesitate to petition the principal, superintendent, and board of education for what they perceived as adequate plan fulfillment. There was never any of this, "Yes, boss," mentality displayed by any of my staff in any of the four school districts for which I have worked.

Although it has not always been pleasant, I have always admired and respected my staff for having the guts to stand up and defend what they believed was right and in the best interest of their students. It is not only their right, but it becomes there professional obligation to do whatever they can to make sure the educational needs of their students are met. In the final analysis, the classroom teacher is the only hope our young people will ever have for adequate self-preparedness for life.

One of my University of Missouri psychology professors stated to the entire class, "You people just sit up here and write down on paper everything I say without ever raising a single question. Your behavior is like that of a class full of puppets with no independent minds of their own." Some of us started speaking up and asking questions. Our professor was elated. We were constantly engaged in a series of debates on any subject of our choice. Our teacher was not as much concerned about right and wrong answers as he was about our ability to take a stand on a particular issue and defend it. He would often raise questions on issues he hoped we would have little or no information on and insist that we offer an opinion. The minute we gave an opinion, the professor would snap back, "Why did you say that?" At this point, we would have to defend our opinion.

Some of us started speaking up and raising questions in other classes and got into trouble immediately. One of my teachers contacted this debating professor and demanded, "What in the world are you teaching these students? That Lemmon Stevenson is constantly questioning and challenging everything I say and do. His behavior is becoming obnoxious." I was advised to cool it for a while and told that it may not be in my best interest to upset too many professors.

One of the most profound benefits I received from the debates was that it forced me to retake the National Teachers Examination resulting in a change of my South Carolina teaching certificate from a B to an A. Prior to the debate, I was happy and extremely grateful that my teaching certificate was a B rather than a C. I knew many C certificate teachers who were much smarter and had a much better education than I had. Accordingly, I was allowing complacency to dominate my thinking and action pertaining to psychological testing. The bottom line is that every human being has the obligation and the indisputable responsibility to use, to the fullest possible extent, the God-given knowledge, wisdom, intelligence, and understanding.

Another benefit I received from our debates was the commitment, courage, and determination to do action research on psychological testing in all of my schools. My conclusion is that the American boy and American girl, regardless of race or state, can do anything they set their minds to, and they can do it just as well if not better than anybody else in the whole world. It is the duty and responsibility of every professional teacher and administrator to do whatever is necessary to teach and help every child to know and understand this essential fact.

Chapter Twenty

A Medley of Invigorating Memories

*P*resident Richard M. Nixon said, "Others will hate you, but when they hate you, they don't win unless you hate them back; and then you destroy yourself." I fully agree with this statement. People will not only hate you but they will say and do mean and evil things to you. They may even kill you. However, there is always a bright side. The Bible declares that we are blessed when men hate us, and we should rejoice and "leap for joy." The only requirement of us is to follow the golden rule and pray for those who hate and despitefully use us.

This chapter will expose you to thirty-four pleasant and unpleasant memories (experiences) in my life and I am pleased to inform you that the worst of these experiences have already rewarded me beyond human imagination.

)())())()(

On August 31, 1991, I officially retired from the Pottstown School District, which brought to a close the 45 year personal adventure I had enjoyed in the field of education. Although I have little or no respect for the word can't, and I do not recall ever backing away from anything I believed was right and in the best interest of children, most of the major projects appeared to be extremely difficult, if not impossible. Individual and group support, however, were always present.

Interestingly, all of my major failures and disappointments (and I have experienced several) have been small and insignificant goals. My big problems and goals, such as finishing college with no money, bringing honor, respectability, comfort, and pride to my adopted Stewart family, helping to meet the educational needs of thousands of young people (with or without their cooperation and support) and writing an inspirational self-esteem book to be shared with the world, have been miraculously successful. Accordingly, we should avoid wasting our precious time and efforts on small insignificant goals and objectives. Go for the sun! Should we find it necessary, after exhausting every possible effort to succeed, to settle for the moon or maybe a star, we will still have accomplished "the impossible."

The following memories, which include the good, bad, ugly, and indifferent, have not only served as a recipe for my successes, but they have also provided me the ultimate challenge of success.

1. "I know you are not dumb or stupid but if you do not start using your brain, you are going to be left behind. Your reading is terrible!"

> Miss Margaret Johnson (My Cousin and
> Second Grade Teacher, 1937)

2. "Lemmon, you must cope with all of the problems, obstacles, and frustrations confronting us all in addition to a whole lot more. You will need to be extremely well trained."

> Professor W. W. Carpenter,
> University of Missouri, 1958

3. "Pertaining to the legacy, 'Give them hell, Harry,' I do not give anybody hell. I simply tell the truth and they think it is hell."

U.S. President Harry S. Truman, 1945-1953

4. "I do not like this boy Lemmon Stevenson. His work in my chemistry class is totally unacceptable and the work he is doing in this dining hall is unsatisfactory. I will tell him the cost of room and board at this college and he will have to pay it from now on."

South Carolina State College Professor and
also Director of the College Dining Hall
(She was also totally anti-Lemmon
Stevenson) Orangeburg, S.C.,1948

5. "Are you going to treat her right?" These were the words spoken by my father-in-law, Professor W. A. Ross, when I asked his permission to marry his daughter, Cecile.

Winnsboro, South Carolina, 1952

6. I told a committee of top administrators and professors at the University of Missouri that I was eternally grateful to them for allowing me the opportunity to attend their honorable and prestigious university. I would love to pursue and earn the Ph.D. degree. However, my major reason for attending your university is to get a good education. The Dean of the School of Education said, "I wish everybody had that much sense."

Dean Loran G. Townsend,
School of Education, 1959

7. "Lemmon, I did not know I required that much work of this class. You will get an 'A' this time."

Professor and Director of Pupil Personnel
Services - University of Missouri, 1959

8. "You really are stupid and a total misfit at this university."

Missouri University Professor (who was
totally anti-Lemmon Stevenson, 1959)

9. "We will see to it that you get the training you need here at this university. You have done a remarkable job."

Dr. Lois Knowles,
Missouri University Professor - 1959

10. "Lemmon, you write very well. You have a good vocabulary and you use it well. However, you are having some difficulty with sentences and paragraph structure. You may wish to stop by my office for a little help. Your writing style is natural, and I love it."

Professor A. Stern Artley, Senior Author
for Scott-Foresman Publishing Co. and
Head of the Reading Dept. at the University of Missouri - 1959

11. The chairman of my Missouri University Advisory Committee, along with two other professors, myself, and three other students attended a workshop in Kansas City, Missouri. On our way back to the University of Missouri, we stopped for dinner at a very nice restaurant. My advisor informed me, as we entered the restaurant, "Lemmon, you can't do this back in Carolina."

We were directed to a large table, served water, and we were in the process of making our orders when the supervisor came over to our table and said to me, "Sir, we cannot serve you in here."

My advisor yelled, "If he cannot eat, then we won't eat!" We all left without eating. I was the only black in the group.

Fall - 1961

12. "Mr. Stevenson, don't worry about your secretary and do not try to do everything yourself. Select individual members of your administrative and teaching staff and place them in charge of major projects or responsibilities and hold them accountable for results."

Mr. Fred L. Fowler, City Superintendent
Greenville School District - 1965

13. "Pertaining to a common sense approach to life, never allow it to be said of you that you were born, you lived, and you died. Do something! If you are ever in doubt about what to do, observe what you see the wisest, best, and richest people in your community, state, and nation do. Do that and it is highly unlikely that you will ever go wrong."

Lemmon Stevenson
Greenville, South Carolina, 1965

14. "Boy, you had better be careful how you fish from the bank of this lake because you just might fall in and wash some of that chocolate off of you."

One white "thoughtful" observer,
Greenville, South Carolina - 1970

15. "Lemmon, you are too ambitious and progressive."

Greenville School District Central
Administrator, 1971

16. Remarks: "Mr. Stevenson made a very favorable impression on me when I knew him at the University of Missouri several years ago. He was in an elementary curriculum course at the graduate level which I was then teaching. In spite of a very limited early school education, he had worked his way up to graduate school. His belief in the benefits and power of education was quite evident, and I admire his perseverance. I believe that he would exert good leadership among students and colleagues."

> Dr. Lois Knowles, Professor Emeritus of
> Education, University of Missouri, 1972

17. "My real estate agent spent one full day with that Lemmon Stevenson family, showing him houses all over the Pottstown area. He bought a house in Pottstown and we did not get one nickel in commission!"

A School District Board Member said, "It is your own fault! You did not show Mr. Stevenson the house he purchased because the house was in an exclusive white community."

The agent told us that the home owners were in Florida, and he would be unable to show the house. Five minutes after the real estate agent left us, we went to the house and bought it from the owners directly.

> Pottstown - June 1972

18. "The Pottstown School District went to a whole lot of trouble bringing you up here to oppress us white folk."

On the second day of school, 1972, one of my white students went home with a bloody nose and a busted lip. His mother assumed that the damage had been done by another black student. She later found out that her son had been attacked by a group of white students. She visited my office the next day and apologized for her attitude.

A disgruntled but fair and responsible parent. Pottstown, 1972

19. "Always remember others will hate you, but when they hate you, they do not win unless you hate them back, and then, you destroy yourself."

Former President Richard Nixon
August 8, 1974

20. "Bringing you to Pottstown was a good move. We want you. You have made it!"

Dr. Ray E. Feick, Superintendent
Pottstown School District - 1976

21. "I think Lemmon Stevenson is the most sincere administrator in this area."

Editor of the Pottstown Mercury - 1976

22. "That Lemmon Stevenson will never back down on anything, especially if he thinks he is right. If you knock him down, he will be back."

Central School Official Pottstown, Pennsylvania - 1981

23. "Somebody said it couldn't be done: But, he with a chuckle replied, 'Maybe it couldn't, but he would be one who wouldn't say so until he had tried.' So, he buckled down and started to work. He started to sing as he tackled the thing that couldn't be done, and he did it."

Author Unknown

There are still those who will say to you, your children, and your grandchildren, you can't do that! Or at least no one else has ever done it. You will fail for sure. With courage, determination, and hope in your heart, tackle the thing that cannot be done, and you will do it.

Lemmon Stevenson

24. *How To Tell a Winner From a Loser*
When a winner makes a mistake, he says, "I was wrong." When a loser makes a mistake, he says, "It wasn't my fault." A winner works harder than a loser and has more time; a loser is always too busy to do what is necessary. A winner makes commitments; a loser makes promises. A winner says, "I am good, but not as good as I ought to be;" a loser says, "I am not as bad as a lot of other people." A winner listens; a loser just waits for his turn to speak. A winner respects his superior and tries to learn from him; a loser resents his superior and tries to find chinks in his armor. A winner feels responsible for more than his job; a loser says, "I just work here." A winner says, "There ought to be a better way to do it;" a loser says, "That is the way we have always done it."

Recipe for Success or Failure
You make the choice. Pottstown, PA
Author Unknown - 1982

25. "I know some of my bosses will be yelling at me, but I am going to help you anyway. You are one of our best customers."

Helen Ketner, Branch Manager, Continental Bank Pottstown, Pennsylvania, 1989

26. "Lemmon, I admire you - being a black man, you have done well. God has blessed you, and He will continue to take care of you."

Senator and Attorney John A. Martin
Winnsboro, South Carolina - 1990

27. "Lemmon, you are too pushy!"

Administrator, Central Administrative
Office, Pottstown, 1990

28. "You have been a vital force in the Pottstown community."

Director of the Pottstown YWCA - 1991

29. "That is why black people in the South no longer have any land. The land was taken from them illegally or, like what is happening to you, shrewd, fee greedy lawyers are dividing and conquering the ignorant, greed, hate, backwardness, and thoughtlessness of potential heirs and create a split in families. In reality, it is a form of a conspiracy to force a land sale. And it is not just happening to black people. It is done under the disguise of helping the poor, defenseless heirs to receive their fair and rightful benefits or share of the property."

A Howard University Law School Graduate and Friend - 1993

30. "I have always found him to be straightforward and fair. You always knew what was on his mind because he would tell you. I have never had another principal like him."

Former English Teacher of the J. E. Beck School, Greenville, South Carolina - 1994

31. "Henretta Stewart and I are the stones that were rejected by the builders and have since become the head of the corner. I was the least intelligent member of the Stevenson

family, and Henretta was the least intelligent of the Stewart family. We are, nonetheless, speaking out for justice and righteousness and we are being heard. The wrongness, evil, and vicious injustice of our Fairfield County, South Carolina, property lawsuit is so profound that if we do not speak out, the stones would immediately cry out."

> Based on Saint Luke 20:17 and Saint Luke
> 19:40 -Lemmon Stevenson, 1995

32. Pertaining to a dream of walking along the beach with God, a man is alleged to have noticed sometimes there was only one set of footprints and that this happened at the lowest and saddest times of his life. "Father," the man said to God, "You said, when I decided to follow you, you would walk with me all the way. Yet, during my most troubled days, there is only one set of footprints. I don't understand why, when I needed you most, you would leave me." The Lord replied, "My precious child, I love you and I would never leave you. During your time of trial and suffering when you saw only one set of footprints, it was then that I carried you."

> Donated to me by Ms. Elaine M. Botton
> Regional Representative, PA Public
> School Retirement Official, July 1995

33. "I am convinced, beyond a reasonable doubt, that our young people are the best, and they deserve the best because they are the only future this nation has. They must be taught how to set meaningful goals and take necessary risks to achieve them. The worst risk in the world is to take no risk. Young people must learn how to cherish and take full advantage of their opportunities and avoid bellyaching and complaining about all of their problems, blaming others,

and trying to get something for nothing. Five plus four equals nine, base ten, for all humans, regardless of race, nationality, or gender."

Lemmon Stevenson, 1995

34. Wisdom for All

The greatest puzzle . . . Life
The greatest invitation of the devil . . . War
The greatest thought . . . God
The most expensive indulgence . . . Hate
The greatest sin . . . Fear
The greatest thing, bar none, in all the world . . . Love
The most ridiculous asset . . . Pride
The best play . . . Work
The greatest mystery . . . Death
The best day . . . Today
The richest asset . . . Health
The greatest stumbling block . . . Egotism
The most dangerous person . . . The Liar
The greatest mistake . . . Giving Up
The cheapest and easiest thing to do . . . Finding Fault
The greatest secret of production . . . Saving Waste
The best work . . . What You Like
The greatest need . . . Common Sense
The most disagreeable person . . . The Complainer
The best town . . . Where you succeeded
The greatest troublemaker . . . One who talks too much
The greatest deceiver . . . One who deceives himself
The biggest fool . . . The Child Who Will Not Go to School
The best teacher . . . One Who Makes You Want to Learn

Author Unknown
Pottstown, Pennsylvania - 1980

Chapter Twenty-one

The Significance of Three Mountaintops

R eaching the top of a major mountaintop, in all of its glory, excitement and splendor, separate and apart from the insurmountable obstacles, struggles, setbacks, and disappointments, is as elusive as searching for tomorrow or as endeavoring to see and catch the wind. True and honorable courage, determination, fulfillment, and strength comes from the struggle involved in reaching the mountaintop. The mountaintop is not an end but a preparation for a new beginning. Also, the struggle is continuous from the cradle to the grave—with no time out.

)(<)(<)(<)(

My first mountaintop of being accepted as a freshman at South Carolina State College was, in reality, the beginning of another four years of intensive struggle to earn a Bachelor of Science degree (B.S.). The moment I earned a college degree, the struggle became even more intensive to secure and succeed in a job in my chosen profession.

The ultimate and truly utopian assignment I received as the first principal of Joseph E. Beck Junior-Senior High School, located in the city of Greenville, South Carolina, was considered the "end" for me. I felt I had finally made it. I wanted Beck to survive forever. What in the world could ever be greater than this? Unfortunately, change is a certainty and nothing lasts forever. The glory and mountaintop celebration was immediately interrupted and curtailed with the reality that I had to recruit, organize, and develop the most efficient and effective teaching staff and junior-senior high school curriculum in the state of South Carolina in only two years.

Our staff, students, and parents allowed themselves to be shackled with the determination to make Beck School the most competitive in this nation, regardless of race. The risk taking and most ambitious goal was designed to derail any notion that Beck School was inferior to white schools, solely because our students and staff were black.

Being the first black principal in the Pottstown School District was a glorious and honorable occasion. My family and I enjoyed the most elaborate, bi-racial reception of our lives. I was and truly enjoyed being a privileged character. However, the honeymoon was short-lived. The profound pressures, struggles, challenges, and obstacles involved in competing favorably with other administrators in the Pottstown area and the state of Pennsylvania were more intense than ever before. John Dewey's contention that education is growth and we must all grow in order that we may continue to grow some more, is the indisputable truth.

Also, life is sharing experiences and its struggle is continuous from the cradle to the grave. In addition, no one ever fully arrives. There is always something else to accomplish. The farther we progress in life, the more intense the struggle becomes. Abraham Lincoln died preparing for the next mountaintop in his administration, which included, "binding up the nations wounds" and promoting love, goodwill, hope, and prosperity between the North and South. His legacy, however, continues.

Franklin Delano Roosevelt died preparing for the next mountaintop in his administration, which included defeating the German and Japanese armies and restoring peace and prosperity to our country and the world. His legacy continues. John F. Kennedy died preparing for his next mountaintop, which included getting re-elected as President of the United States and bringing peace to this nation and the world. His legacy continues.

Martin Luther King, Jr., died preparing for his next mountaintops which included economic, political, and social equality between whites and blacks. Also, love, brotherhood, acceptance, and deliverance of all human beings. His legacy continues. Moses died in the struggle to lead his people to the promised land. His legacy continues. Jesus Christ died preparing for his next mountaintop, which included carrying his message of love, hope, humility, prosperity, redemption, and deliverance to the chosen Jewish people and also to all human beings worldwide. His legacy continues.

There is no free lunch or free ride on life's journey. There is no respecter of persons, no welfare or affirmative action or quotas and, in the end, the playing field is leveled and everybody, regardless of social-economic status, race, nationality, or gender, pays the piper. The fact that our true joy, glory, and honor in this life comes from loving and serving other humans, it is imperative that we learn to love and serve others if for no other reason than self-preservation. Hate destroys the hater. Our love and consideration for the goodwill of others should be so profound that we would be ashamed to die before having done everything we possibly could to help build a better America.

If you are reading this book, it means that my fourth mountaintop will have been accomplished which allows me the opportunity to share my life experiences with boys, girls, men, and women of this nation in order that they may be helped with the lessons of life that I have learned. My mountaintop obstacle courses have insured me countless numbers of blessings, and I am convinced, beyond a reasonable doubt, that this book can and will be an indisputably inspiring blessing to you and anyone else who will dare read it and follow its lead. We were all born to succeed, not fail. Also, like happiness, success has always been one of our basic desires.

Many people have written about success in many different ways, but the rules have never changed and they never will. Most people are about as happy and successful as they make up their minds to be. All you have to do is to make up your mind what it is you want to do and then work at it as hard as you possibly can. You have to be positive and you have to believe in yourself. You really can do it if you try. Never give up. Set your goals, take the high road, go for it and never, never look back!

The following obnoxious and destructive woes are to be condemned and eradicated:

• The "Cannot Do" Mentality.

A natural, inborn, spirituality existing in every human being is constantly saying to you and me, "You definitely can do anything you set your mind to. All you have to do is to be willing to pay the supreme price of total commitment, perseverance, and persistence."

• Profound and Uncontrollable Fear.

Fear is and always has been, without question, the greatest sin known to man. When allowed to penetrate freely through the hearts and minds of human beings, they can easily become incapacitated. The courage, willpower, determination, and perseverance necessary to function successfully in any goal or routine daily activities can and will be destroyed. I shall never forget my first coast-to-coast airplane flight. I was intensely and uncontrollably fearful of dying from an airplane crash.

• **Excessive Greed and the Selfish "Me, Myself, and I" Mentality.**

Excessive greed and selfishness can very easily destroy any hope of happiness or self-fulfillment. The more the greedy person gets the more he wants. He or she is so busy serving self that there is never time or available resources to share with others. Service to our fellowman is the foundation for true happiness and fulfillment.

• **The "Play It Safe" or "No Risk" Mentality.**

The only certainty life has to offer is risk. Everything we do involves some degree of risk. My mother risked death in the process of giving me life. She also risked my life and future by placing me in the hands of her best friend when I was only five months old. Every time we climb a flight of stairs, we face the risk of falling and suffering injury. Every time we open our mouths to speak we face the risk of being misunderstood, saying the wrong thing, or being severely criticized for our beliefs or convictions.

Irresponsibilities which include, but by no means limited to, shiftlessness, thoughtlessness, unreliable, wildness, backwardness, laziness, ignorant, stupid, evilness, viciousness, injustice, envy, jealousy, moaning and groaning, blaming others for all of our troubles, and also a high concentration of the nigger mentality.

Although irresponsibility and name calling of any description have no place in our society, the word nigger has long, strong, and apparently indestructible roots that extend all the way back to Abraham Lincoln and slavery; however, its true meaning has never changed and it never will. White and black citizens are just as much offended by the word in 1997 as they were on January 1, 1863, when Abraham Lincoln signed the Emancipation Proclamation, which declared all American slaves were free. The feud that erupted on national television, when one attorney introduced the word into the famous 1995 O.J. Simpson Trial, is only one concrete example. Taped conversations of ex-detective Mark Fuhrman, in which the word is constantly used, is another example. Fuhrman talks about killing niggers and that female officers don't do anything. The word has become synonymous with racism.

Not only am I very comfortable and not threatened or offended by the word, I have been a real indisputable nigger on many more occasions than I care to admit and I did not travel that path alone. This country has always had an ample supply of niggers. However, the glory and honor of it is that I have a clear, concise, true, realistic perception of what constitutes a nigger and I have been able to use it most effectively in accomplishing meaningful and constructive goals for myself and hundreds of other young people in South Carolina and Pennsylvania. Many of those honorable achievers are now located in other states throughout this nation.

Even though the concept is still alive and well today, we all have freedom of choice. I utilize to the fullest extent the old saying, *sticks and stones may break my bones, but words don't bother me.* Also, the fact that any human being, regardless of race, nationality, or gender, can be a nigger, the concept can and definitely should be discussed openly and considered in a modern realistic view. Niggerism is not limited to blacks and it should never be confused with the word Negro, which refers to men and women of color. My final words on the issue: If the shoe fits, wear it.

• The Fear of Death.

Death, in its place and time, is to be considered as a welcomed friend. It is not and never has been bad. It is normal, natural, and just as much a part of life as being born. Death is no respecter of persons. It does not care what your age is, who your parents are, how much money you have, or how famous you may be. In due time, death comes to every living creature. God is in charge of birth and death and no one is born or dies before his/her time.

Although God does not bother to tell us the exact date we will die, I submit to you that the only thing to fear pertaining to your death is that perhaps you may not do everything that you possibly can, on a daily basis, to help make this world a better place in which to live. Remember, you are not free and you will never be free as long as you fear death. It has been said and I agree that maybe God wilfully and deliberately shields from us the glory and honor of death for fear of our hurrying up and dying in order to enjoy the glory of death, rather than remain here on earth and complete our God-given mission.

A funeral sermon entitled, *Go Down Death* by Dr. James Weldon Johnson, 1871-1938, helps place the above contention in perspective.

Day before yesterday morning,
God was looking down from His great, high heaven,
Looking down on all His children
And His eyes fell on Sister Caroline,
Tossing on her bed of pain.
And God's big heart was touched with pity,
With the everlasting pity.
And God said: Go down, Death, go down,
Go down to Savannah, Georgia,
Down in Yamacraw,
And find Sister Caroline.
She's borne the burden and heat of the day,
She's labored long in my vineyard,
And she's tired -

She's weary -
Go down, Death, and bring her to Me.

While we were watching round her bed,
She turned her eyes and looked away,
She saw what we couldn't see;
She saw Old Death. She saw Old Death,
Coming like a falling star.
But Death didn't frighten Sister Caroline;
He looked to her like a welcome friend.
And she whispered to us: I'm going home,
And she smiled and closed her eyes.

And Death took her up like a baby,
And she lay in his icy arms,
But she didn't feel no chill.
And Death began to ride again -
Up beyond the evening star,
Out beyond the morning star,
Into the glittering light of glory,
On to the Great White Throne.
And there he laid Sister Caroline
On the loving breast of Jesus.

And Jesus took His own hand and
wiped away her tears,
And He smoothed the furrows from her face,
And the angels sang a little song,
And Jesus rocked her in His arms,
And kept a-saying: Take your rest,
Take your rest, take your rest.

Weep not - weep not,

She is not dead;
She's resting in the bosom of Jesus.
Heart-broken husband - weep no more;
Grief-stricken son - weep no more;
Left-lonesome daughter - weep no more;
She's only just gone home."

The following virtues and humanitarian deeds are to be endorsed and pursued with maximum vigor:

• Always strive for high, exemplary expectations and goals. This is the only known way to get ahead on any important mission. We must always believe in and work for the best and, if necessary, expect a miracle.

• Action based on **today** is essential for the achieving of any meaningful and important goal. Never put off for tomorrow what you can and should do today. Yesterday is gone and tomorrow is not promised. However, we do have today. If we will do the very best job we possibly can with whatever obligations and responsibilities we encounter today, we will not have to worry about tomorrow. Nothing in this whole world can ever be more destructive to our dreams, plans, goals, and objectives than procrastination.

• Formal education is powerful, essential, and a must for all human beings. Therefore, we must all get as much of it as we possibly can. Educational opportunities for all Americans are greater than ever before. Also, ignorance is, without doubt, the greatest destructive force in this nation and the world. Our formal educational training should be a minimum of high school through college. If this writer could earn formal education through Graduate School during the 50's, it is a cinch that you will be able to do it in the 90's. Further, most racism throughout this nation and the world is saturated with ignorance.

• Always take love over hate and provide meaningful and essential services designed to help ensure success and freedom for your fellow man. Love, respect, receptiveness, and human services to our fellow man in a society which glories in putting others down is extremely difficult. It is so much easier to criticize, condemn, and endeavor to destroy others. Hate, which is a known indisputable self-destroyer, is always lurking in the hearts of man. The temptation to hate can easily become overbearing. The blues singer B.B. King says it best in the song, "Nobody Loves Me But My Mama and Sometimes I Think She Is Jiving, Too."

• Always give to the world the best that you have and the best will come back to you. In all truth, we brought nothing into this world, and we know of no one in the history of this world who has ever carried anything out of it. Therefore, the accumulation of material goods, finances, and services, solely and specifically for selfish reasons, represents the wisdom and understanding of a hoarding fool. We should definitely accumulate as much money and other materials as we possible can and use it to help provide essential services to ourselves and also to less fortunate humans - especially young people who represent the only future this nation has. You must make money for yourself because it is impossible to help others if you are in no position to help yourself. Most importantly, it is impossible to give more to humanitarian causes than you will receive in return.

• Stand up, speak up, promote, and defend vigorously whatever is right, honorable, essential, and in the best interest of our young people - statewide and nationally. For example, parents and citizens of every public school district throughout this nation should demand concrete, indisputably objective, equitable accountability of its effectiveness with our young people. (This is especially true and important at the primary level in the areas of reading, math, English, writing, speaking, social studies, and physical fitness. The most effective and efficient way to accomplish this is through standardized testing in which the Bell Curve is fully utilized.

The very best classical literature, in which the whole language approach, using whole, non-censored authentic pieces of literature, has been defined and documented as the most meaningful and effective method of meeting the reading needs of all students grades K-8 on an equitable basis. The value of whole language is not new for it has been utilized in the very best and most prestigious schools throughout this nation and the world for years. Thanks to the commitment and aggressive production and promotion of the whole language concept by the Houghton-Mifflin publication company, during the 80's and 90's, it is making a significant comeback in our public schools. I contend that whole language can and should be made a part of every public school curriculum, throughout this nation and the world. It is imperative that pure literature be taught to all of our young people on a systematic basis. Fragmented censored literature has no place in future school curriculums.)

• Mental and physical fitness are essentials for all human beings, regardless of race, age, or nationality. Adults should walk or run three miles three or four times per week and also meditate, in which deep breathing is utilized, for 15 or 20 minutes, three to four times per week. Essential longevity mental and physical therapeutic benefits can be achieved no other way.

• Let not your hearts be troubled when other humans deceive

you, lie to you, endeavor to destroy you, or display total contempt or threats of total destruction of a righteous cause or humanitarian deed you are promoting. Instead, use their opposition, roadblocks, and obstacles as building blocks to help ensure the success of your mission. If your mission is righteous and truly Godly, more than ample support necessary for its success is guaranteed. You cannot possibly lose. Much of your support could come from anonymous or unexpected sources. However, you must believe in yourself and you must be positive. The power of positive thinking is unlimited and immeasurable.

• Let not your hearts be troubled <u>ever</u>; because the God that is in me and you is more than sufficient to protect and sustain you through any obstacles, malicious, evil, or vicious attacks this world can level against you - including death.

• Always hope for the best, plan for the best, work for the best, but, in the end, be prepared to deal effectively with whatever occurs. Do not allow yourself to become dismayed when things go wrong with your plans. Always maintain your hope, courage, and determination to stay on course and press on. What do we do when hope is gone? This day we press on and on and on! The poem *Columbus* by Hiner Miller (1841-1913) summed it up beautifully in, "What shall we do when hope is gone?" The words leaped like a leaping sword: "Sail on! Sail on! Sail on! and on!"

• **Never, never, never** retire. If you enjoy and love your work, stay with it until death do we part. If you hate your work, leave it as soon as possible for another suitable job. Although I have not always believed this, work is the most important single blessing this world has to offer. Babcock (1858-1901) said it best in his poem, *Be Strong.*

"Be strong! We are not here to play, to dream, to drift; we have hard work to do, and loads to lift; shun not the struggle—face it; 'tis God's gift."

Epilogue

I t is imperative that every human being be directed and guided into asking the following questions: Who am I? Where did I come from? Where am I going? These questions should be answered in a positive and constructive manner.

My own answers to these questions are: I am somebody. I am one of the most important and uniquely created human beings that ever lived. God created me and He created you and all other human beings worldwide. We are endowed with a powerful and miraculously unlimited spirituality that will make it possible for us to be or become anything we set our minds too. All we have to do is clarify in our minds specifically what it is that we wish to accomplish and then work at it as hard as we possibly can.

There is no other human being in the world who is exactly like me and there is no other human in the world who can do what I do exactly the way I do it. The cue here is to become a doer. If you are having difficulty setting meaningful and essential humanitarian goals, you should observe, read and study what the wisest and most responsible people of this world are doing. Then, do that, and it is highly unlikely that you will go wrong.

I am saddened by the biblical story which alleges that

Methuselah lived for 969 years. As a result of his longevity, all anyone has ever been able to say about him is that he was born, he lived, and he died! What a tragic waste of precious time and unlimited opportunities.

Who am I? I am a doer created in the image of God! I am highly experienced with obstacles, hardships, and poverty. I am experienced in the social, political, and classicism isolation by blacks and whites. I am also fully aware of the reality that white people can be much more oppressive, evil, and vicious toward other whites than they have been toward blacks. Much of what black people call white racism is simply business as usual.

My professional credentials classify me as a professionally licensed barber, an elementary school teacher, an elementary principal, a high school principal, and a public school superintendent for the state of South Carolina. I have actually served in all of the above capacities, except superintendent.

Where did I come from? I was born, reared, educated, and worked in South Carolina during the late 1920s and 1960s. In 1972, at the age of 44, my family and I moved to Pottstown, PA. After serving as Principal, Director of Federal Programs, and Central Office Administrator, I retired in 1991.

Where am I going? I shall continue traveling the path of truth, freedom, justice, love, and humanitarian services to others, especially young people. I shall follow the path of education, wisdom, and responsibility. I will honor and respect love over hate and I will condemn and do everything in my power to help eradicate ignorance, irresponsibility, and the lazy "something for nothing" dead beat mentality. This free loading mentality is too prevalent in the hearts and minds of many Americans.

Where am I going? I am going to achieve true and meaningful self-fulfillment by helping to establish, in the hearts and minds of thousands of individuals, the priority goals of good health, education, unlimited and continuous service to our fellow man.

Appendix

Beck High School and Middle School Scholarship Fund
By
Lemmon Stevenson, first principal
Rudolph Gordan, second principal and
current Superintendent of the Greenville School District
Larry King, current principal
Susan S. Jones, former teacher
Ernest Hamilton, former student, lawyer, and Assistant
District Attorney
Jim Bridges, business manager
June 2, 1997

This scholarship fund, established June 2, 1997, by two former principals, one current principal, one teacher, Superintendent of Schools, former student, and business manager, is supported by faculty, former students, and parents of the Beck attendance area. The fund is designed to serve as an unique and powerful student motivator for all current and future Beck School District attendance area students, regardless of race. The award is based upon innovative projects which produced outstanding student accomplishments at Beck High School between 1965 and 1972. Many of these honorable students are doctors, lawyers, professional speech writers, entertainers, teachers, ministers, earned Ph.D. business executives, principals, and other humanitarian servants. The scholarship project shows appreciation for their commitments along with, pride, honor, and respect for their accomplishments.

Specifically, our mission is to make absolutely certain that every student in the Beck School attendance area knows and understands that he/she can be real winners at being and doing anything they set their minds too. However, students must set high goals, be positive and demonstrate sufficient effort to reach them. They must never give up. Winners never quit and quitters never win!

The awards will be paid directly to the college or vocational trade school in which the winning students will have enrolled. The amount of the award will be determined by the interest earned on the principle of this tax deductible scholarship fund, for the year the award is given. The scholarships will be issued on behalf of three Beck Middle School graduates, who demonstrate the highest degree of mastery and utilization of the following guidelines and good citizenship principles:

1. Must spend three full years at the Beck Middle School, (Grades 6, 7, and 8) before graduation. Students will be identified as winners upon completing eighth grade.

However, before they will enjoy benefits of the scholarship, they will be required to complete high school and become a freshman in a college or trade school.

2. Must demonstrate a positive and constructive attitude about school work and also his/her relationships with teachers and other students.

3. Must demonstrate responsibility for his/her behavior during the school day and also on the way to and from school. (Self-Discipline)

4. Must demonstrate necessary courage and perseverance to work on extremely challenging tasks, and if failure occurs, be willing to start again and work harder to achieve success. (Never give up.)

5. Must be academically competitive with other students at the local, state, and national levels, as measured by psychological standardized tests. Student's overall school grades must be good to superior.

6. Must demonstrate commitment and determination to serve others (potential humanitarian).

The student selection will be done by the appropriate classroom teachers, the guidance counselor, and the building principal.

The fund, which is open for tax deductible contributions from teachers, administrators, former students, parents, community, and anyone else willing to contribute, is expected to exceed $100,000. The initial fund pledges are $5,000.00. Contributions to the fund at this time are sincerely appreciated. The fund will be invested and only the interest will be awarded to qualifying students.

Checks should be made payable to "The School District of Greenville County-Beck Scholarship Fund," 301 Camperdown Way, P.O. Box 2848, Greenville, S.C. 29602-2848.

Mitford Elizabeth Heights
School Scholarship Fund

By
Lemmon Stevenson, Former teacher and principal
B.B. Washington, Former teacher and principal
Melvina Moore, former teacher
Gaither Bumgardner, executive principal
Doug Broome, business manager
June 3, 1997

This scholarship fund, established June 3, 1997, by two former principals, one teacher, executive principal and business manager, is supported by faculty, former students, and parents of the Mitford and Elizabeth Height School area. The fund is designed to serve as a unique and powerful student motivator for all current and future Great Falls attendance area students, regardless of race. The award is based upon innovative projects which produced outstanding student accomplishments at Mitford and Elizabeth Heights between 1956 and 1965. Many of these honorable students are teachers, ministers, earned Ph.D. business executives, principals, and other humanitarian servants. The scholarship project shows appreciation for their commitments, along with pride, honor, and respect for their accomplishments.

Specifically, our mission is to make absolutely certain that every student in the Great Falls attendance area knows and understands that he/she can be real winners at being and doing anything they set their minds too. However, students must set high goals, be positive and demonstrate sufficient effort to reach them. They must never give up. Winners never quit and quitters never win!

The awards will be paid directly to the college or vocational trade school in which the winning students will have enrolled. The amount of the award will be determined by the interest earned on the principle of this tax deductible scholarship funds for the year the award is given. The scholarships will be issued on behalf of three Great Falls Senior High School graduates, who demonstrate the highest degree of mastery and utilization of the following guidelines and good citizenship principles:

1. Must spend at least three years at the Great Falls Senior High School, (Grades 10, 11, and 12) before graduation.

2. Must demonstrate a positive and constructive attitude about school work and also his/her relationships with teachers and other students.

3. Must demonstrate responsibility for his/her behavior during the school day and also on the way to and from school. (Self-Discipline)

4. Must demonstrate necessary courage and perseverance to work on extremely challenging tasks, and if failure occurs, be willing to start again and work harder to achieve success. (Never give up.)

5. Must be academically competitive with other students at the local, state, and national levels, as measured by psychological standardized tests. Student's overall school grades must be good to superior.

6. Must demonstrate commitment and determination to serve others (potential humanitarian).

The student selection will be done by the appropriate classroom teachers, the guidance counselor, and the building principal.

The fund, which is open for tax deductible contributions from teachers, administrators, former students, parents, community, and anyone else willing to contribute, is expected to exceed $50,000. The initial fund pledges are $5,000.00. Contributions to the fund at this time are sincerely appreciated. The fund will be invested and only the interest will be awarded to qualifying students.

Checks should be made payable to: The Chester School District, Mitford-Elizabeth Height Scholarship Fund, 109 Hinton Street, Chester, S.C. 29706.